"Personal Power Masteyth
masterpiece that encou

PERSONAL POWER
≡ MASTERY ≡

DOUGLAS VERMEEREN

Personal Power Mastery

First published in 2018 by

Panoma Press Ltd
48 St Vincent Drive, St Albans, Herts, AL1 5SJ, UK
info@panomapress.com
www.panomapress.com

Book layout by Neil Coe.

Printed on acid-free paper from managed forests.

Printed and bound by TJ International Ltd, Padstow, Cornwall

ISBN 978-1-784521-48-6

The right of Douglas Vermeeren to be identified as the author of this work has been asserted in accordance with sections 77 and 78 of the Copyright, Designs and Patents Act 1988.

A CIP catalogue record for this book is available from the British Library.

This book is available online and in bookstores.

Dedication

To My Best Friend Holly

Disclaimer

Although the author and publisher have made every effort to ensure that the information in this book was correct at press time, the author and publisher do not assume and hereby disclaim any liability to any party due to these words coming from the author's own opinion based on his experiences.

Every word in this book is based on the author's own experience of his personal development journey and the outcomes with clients that he may have witnessed. Although we have made every reasonable attempt to achieve complete accuracy in the content of this book, we assume no responsibility for errors or omissions in the information in this book.

You should only use this information as you see fit at your own risk. Your life and circumstances may not be suited to the examples we share within these pages. The author and publisher are neither doctors nor in the position of registered authorities to give you expert advice. All we can share is what we have tested on ourselves and obtained through witnessing the changes in our lives or our clients' lives along the way.

How you choose to use the information in this book within your own life is completely your own responsibility and own risk.

Testimonials

"Douglas Vermeeren has hit this one out of the park. This book is bound to become a classic in personal development literature. A must read if you want to improve your outcomes and shift from average to extraordinary performance in your life."

- Dr. Joe Vitale, author of *The Attract Factor*, *Zero Limits* and featured teacher in *The Secret*

"Doug Vermeeren definitely knows what he's talking about. He's dynamic and wise and definitely worth listening to."

- Marci Shimoff, author of *Chicken Soup for the Woman's Soul*, *Happy for No Reason* and featured teacher in *The Secret*

"Douglas Vermeeren is a great teacher and a visionary who is making a significant difference in the lives of people everywhere."

- Dr. John Demartini, international speaker, leadership and performance specialist and featured teacher in *The Secret*

"Doug is definitely destined to become one of this generation's leaders in personal development."

- Bob Doyle, creator of the Wealth Beyond Reason program and featured teacher in *The Secret*

"Douglas Vermeeren has amazing gifts to bring your life to a whole other level. You will totally fall in love with him."

**- Marie Diamond, Feng Shui expert
and featured teacher in *The Secret***

"Douglas Vermeeren shares some powerful insights into success, achievement and the power you have within you in this dynamic book - Personal Power Mastery. If you want to achieve more and improve your outcomes do yourself a favor and read this book."

**- Dr. Greg Reid, author and speaker,
Think and Grow Rich series**

"When Doug speaks people listen and learn and laugh and want more!"

**- Morris "The Miracle Man Goodman", author, speaker
and featured teacher in *The Secret***

"Doug is truly a go-giver and what you will learn from his principles and acting on them will not only change your life and make you a better person, they will also help you to be a happier individual as you go through life."

**- Richard "Jaws" Kiel, actor,
*The Spy Who Loved Me, Moonraker***

"Definitely check out Douglas Vermeeren. He's excellent! He coached me and really made a huge difference."

-Louie Anderson, legendary comedian

"The very best work with Doug. If you ever have the opportunity to work with Doug, do your future a favor and jump on it now."

**- Kyle Cease, comedian and actor,
winner of the *Comedy Central* stand-up comedy showdown,
10 things I Hate About You and *Not Another Teen Movie***

"Doug Vermeeren is a man who possesses both vision and enthusiasm. He spreads his message of no limits to everyone and touches lives forever."

- Frank Maguire, co-founder Fed Ex

"A unique perspective on success that includes essentials previously overlooked. Douglas Vermeeren's research into top achievers makes Personal Power Mastery one of the most powerful success books written today."

-Stefan Aarnio, award-winning real estate investor and author

"Personal Power Mastery stands above so many of the personal empowerment books today. Jam-packed with effective strategies that you can implement immediately, this book certainly has what it takes to level up from average to extraordinary."

**- Chris Widener, best-selling author
of *The Art of Influence* and *The Angel Inside***

"Douglas Vermeeren is a visionary leader who will help transform your life, grow your business and create personal mastery! No doubt he is destined for greatness and will help propel you to the next level in your own journey."

**- Drew Hunthausen, the No Excuses Blind Guy.
#1 blind motivational speaker, coach, international best-selling author and award-winning triathlete**

"If you're looking to improve your situation and unlock more powerful results in your life you are going to find Personal Power Mastery a valuable book. Douglas Vermeeren shares clear and concise strategies that anyone can apply to achieve more and grow."

**- Barnet Bain, Academy Award winner, director of *Milton's Secret*, producer of *What Dreams May Come*, author of
*The Book of Doing and Being***

"I was part of Douglas Vermeeren's Personal Power Mastery and it rocked my world. He has methods of setting goals and just feeling more powerful that I have never witnessed before and I'm a former professional wrestler! I was engaged every step of the way. You will not only experience personal growth along the way, but you will remember it and use it to create a spectacular life!"

- Rick Titan, WWF professional wrestler

"Do you want to have and experience more 'personal power' in your life? You know, that feeling where you are capable of achieving pretty much anything. If you answered yes, then this book is for you. If you answered no, this book might be the most important book you ever read! Doug Vermeeren shares simple, yet unique and powerful strategies for making lasting changes that are proven to work and get results.

Learning from Doug has changed my life. I wish I had this information when I was still competing as I'm sure it would have helped me achieve significantly more in my sport and it will absolutely for you, if you read it and implement it into your life."

- Jason Parker, Olympic medalist, speaker/trainer and Mastermind leader

Acknowledgements and Gratitude

This is always the hardest part of the book to write for me. As I think back over all of the many people who contributed to the creation of this book and all of the sources and people where I learned elements of this content from, my mind is truly blown away. There are so many powerful people that I have to thank that I am filled with gratitude now even just thinking about it.

For the support in crediting, editing, formatting and publishing of this book I want to thank Mindy Gibbins-Klein and her amazing team at Panoma Press; Heather Andrews and her amazing team at Follow it Thru Publishing: editors Suzanne and Amanda, and Bojan, formatter; and Keith Leon and the gang at Baby Pie Publishing. I also want to thank my personal assistant Rachel Dobson for her efforts.

And now how in the heck do I do this part...? My mission to learn about success began with interviewing more than 400 of the world's top achievers. Each one of them was so inspirational to me in their own way and taught me so much about the success. You'll find their stories and personalities woven so much through the Personal Power Mastery lessons. But how the heck can I list all of the top achievers in the original group of 400 plus all of the incredible people since then? They have all been so amazing to meet and become friends with. You changed my life.

And if you are one of my top achievers reading this – thank you, thank you, thank you. My life has entirely changed because of the amazing difference you have made. I will be grateful to you forever.

Doug

Foreword

Personal Power Mastery is a no-nonsense, experiential growth masterpiece that encourages you to make shifts in your beliefs. Making these shifts will create paradigm shifts in your life. The power thoughts, stories, lessons, exercises and questions to consider presented in this book are inspiring and thought-provoking. This book encourages you to be a doer, not a talker. As Doug shares within the pages of *Personal Power Mastery*, the concepts in the book are simple to read; however, it's the doing that will make the difference in the results you will achieve.

It's amazing what Douglas Vermeeren has created in his life. He's directed and appeared in three inspiring personal development movies, authored books and series, such as *Guerrilla Marketing* and *Amazing Success*. He gets to share his mission and message with rooms filled with people who are perfectly ready to hear his message. Douglas is a walking, talking demonstration of the lessons you'll learn while reading this book.

Having mentors and inspiring books in your life is good, but more importantly, it's what you do with the information that will create change. Doug Vermeeren's life was forever changed by *Think and Grow Rich* by Napoleon Hill, just as mine was. We both learned that repetition and action are what creates a paradigm shift.

In 1961, I met a man named Ray Stanford. I was cleaning offices for a living at that time. He said, "If you do exactly what I tell you, you can have anything you want." I didn't really believe that at the time, but I believed he believed it, and I just made the decision I was going to do what he said. It was strange because I had never done that with anyone before in my life. I was always going in the wrong direction, and anybody who had tried to help me was unsuccessful.

One of the things Ray did was give me a copy of *Think and Grow Rich* and he said, "Read this every day." That was on October 21, 1961. I'm still reading it every day and I carry it everywhere I go. I also listened every day to Earl Nightingale's condensed narration of *Think and Grow Rich*. I couldn't stop listening to it. The repetition of the positive reprogramming was sure making me feel different.

It wasn't long before I had earned over a million dollars in one year. It was almost like a self-realization crisis. I thought, *How in the heck did this happen?* When somebody asked me what I was doing, I would say, "I was cleaning offices." But there were a lot of people cleaning offices that weren't doing what I was doing. I also said, "I'm listening to *Think and Grow Rich*." There were a lot of people reading *Think and Grow Rich* – they weren't doing what I was doing. Then, I thought of all the repetition I had with the book and the recordings. I would listen to the recordings every day; I still do. I still read the book every day, 57 years later. I realized that I had reprogrammed my subconscious mind. I changed my paradigm.

A paradigm is a multitude of habits in the subconscious mind. Our self-image is part of the paradigm, and if that isn't changed, nothing changes. When it does change, everything changes. It doesn't change like throwing on a light switch, it's a process – and through the repetition, everything changes. Once I became clear on why things had changed for me, all I wanted to do was share it with everybody I could. I wanted to teach this to everybody I could reach.

I think Einstein had it down pat. He said that our only purpose being here is to serve. If you're really locked into that, and all you want to do is help, when you see a person get it, it's so rewarding.

In this book, you'll learn about the power of choice, the power of your thoughts, the power of perception and beliefs, the power of change, and the power of mastery. Doing the processes, answering the questions, and more importantly reading this book over and over again will create a shift in your paradigm. Get this information in every form available; repeat the power thoughts over and over again. Repetition is key. I can assure you that if you wear this book out, you will see positive change in your life.

Enjoy the journey,

Bob Proctor
Author, speaker and featured teacher in the hit movie *The Secret*

Contents

Introduction

The concepts in my book are simple. I have a unique system to get the results you are seeking and create the lasting success you deserve.

This work isn't like other personal development books you have read before.

While many of these written guides have excellent information and insights to create the "best you" possible, the way they are composed often leaves a feeling of incompleteness. Most of them are based on theory and the personal experiences of the authors. This book was created much differently, with a higher and deeper vision in mind.

This project began for me when I was attending college. Up until then, I had never really heard of personal development and wasn't even aware of how individuals could change their situations or control the outcomes of their lives. I was raised in a family with low earnings. I wore hand-me-downs and was answered with the word "no" any time I asked for money. My parents worked really hard, but they were always struggling to make ends meet.

I knew it was possible to have greater financial resources because I witnessed friends who had more revenue. Growing up, I assumed that it was really a matter of luck and being born into the right circumstances. I didn't have any big expectations of my life being different from what I had experienced up until that point. Things were the way they were, and I just accepted that.

Then came college, as I stated earlier…

I took a job selling pest control products door-to-door in California over the summer. I worked hard because I grew up under the impression that survival comes as a result of being tough and solid in a position. I worked countless hours that summer. Looking back, I estimate that I knocked on over 22,000 doors in the heat of the California desert. Was it painless? No. Did I have brilliant results? No.

At times, it was discouraging. I remember one particular afternoon I was feeling really disheartened. I wasn't in the mood to go to work. I didn't feel like I was getting any results, and that there was no point continuing. I was on the verge of quitting.

It was at this juncture that a close friend gave me the book *Think and Grow Rich* by Napoleon Hill. To complete his book, Napoleon Hill worked under the influence of Andrew Carnegie and conducted first-hand research and interviews with more than 400 of the world's top achievers in his day. He studied people like Henry Ford, Thomas Edison, Rockefeller, the Wrigleys, and more. As a result, he was able to create several important pieces in personal development literature that have since influenced almost everything that has followed his writings and observations.

When I read *Think and Grow Rich*, I was impressed by many of the powerful lessons within. More than that, I was inspired by Hill's connection to the top achievers and what he learned first-hand. In my mind, I imagined that although much of what he learned was captured, there were many lessons that never made it into the pages of that book. This idea of hidden or secret lessons interested me and intrigued me so much that I determined to start my own mission.

I knew that I couldn't go out and meet many of Napoleon Hill's original top achievers. Most of them passed away before I was even born, so I decided to pursue a calling to personally meet and interview the top achievers of our day.

A major difference from Hill's objectives is that I would not only include business leaders but athletes, celebrities and spiritual leaders as well. I hungered to understand what it was that created their extraordinary success.

My research has led to me connecting with Academy Award winners, Olympic medalists, and founders of some of the larger global brands in existence today. While it has taken over a decade to complete the first 400 interviews to catch up to Napoleon Hill, the results began pouring in almost immediately. I am going to share some of those strategies in this book. However, the real power in these principles came after a second experiment that really sets this volume apart from any other personal development materials I have encountered before mine.

I decided to expand my research into those who were *unable* to create success. That's right. I studied people who encountered patterns of difficulty and challenge. This study included people who had gone through serious failures in life, including bankruptcy, divorce, business failures, and even prison time. What was the difference between those who achieved high levels of success and those who experienced tragedy? I wanted an answer.

Both groups started with hopes, dreams and possibilities. Almost everyone in both groups had goals/plans and thought they were working in a way that would get them positive outcomes and success. They all put forth their best efforts and followed what they thought was the best route. So, what went wrong for some but extremely well for others?

In this volume, I will unfold several of the key differences and point out many of the elements that create incredible success. You will see that they are attainable by all.

Often, it is just the right combination of the little things that makes or breaks the end result.

By teaching these principles to thousands around the globe in my seminars, I have been able to systematize these concepts into a recognizable pattern and sequence. I will share it all with you in a way that you will be able to repeat in practical terms to get the results you are looking for in your life.

For the first time, we will introduce a concept called the five pillars and show how everyone is motivated to achieve in each of these areas.

I want you to get the most out of this book. In my experience, reading alone will not create the changes that most people are looking for. Building on this perspective, I am going to invite you to *not* read this book. (That's probably the first time you've ever had an author suggest that.)

Instead, I want you to *experience* the book and incorporate these lessons into your life in real time. **Think of this book as more of an assignment guide**. If you are serious about your success, you will appreciate this approach much better.

In each chapter, there will be exercises and questions to complete, which will help you to bring the material into your life in a way that it will become yours. You will *become more,* and you will be able to *achieve more.* As you will learn shortly, your growth will not be an event but a process.

For this reason, I will invite you to return to this material often. I recommend reading and experiencing this book once or twice a year and redoing all of the exercises each time. You will find it exciting as you see your answers change and shift to a much higher level of thinking.

In addition, I would invite you to join us at one of our live experiences where we teach you additional strategies and insights on how to incorporate these principles into your daily journey toward success.

Similar to my experiences with *Think and Grow Rich*, there are many great teachable moments that I experienced with the top achievers that were not able to make it into this volume. At the end of this book, I will share some additional resources for you to dive deeper into this content.

Before we get started together, I would like to point out that although you may return to certain chapters in this book to improve specific areas of your life in pursuit of excellence, it is strongly recommended that you read this book through the first time in chronological order. This strategy will give you the lay of the land, so to speak. Once you understand the map, you will be able to select the destinations you would like to visit more accurately.

Finally, I want to thank you for buying this book. Not just for how it helps support me in my mission to teach these principles, but more importantly, for the kind of person you are striving to become. I believe in the idea that the world is made up of individuals, and as individuals we can evolve to a **higher level of thinking and possibility**.

Thank you for helping make where I live a better place.

Sincerely,
Douglas Vermeeren

CHAPTER ONE

What is Personal Power Mastery?

*Once you really commit and decide
to do something, the pieces to get it done
start to appear.*

Douglas Vermeeren

Make success personal

Each lesson is a step closer to mastery

You are better than you think you are

As I sat across from William Farley in his Chicago home, I realized something very interesting about the insights to success I was gaining.

Bill, as he asked me to call him, was best known as the former CEO of Fruit of the Loom underwear. He was not the first top achiever in my study. However, I distinctly remember that this was the point where I had a massive **a-ha moment,** which is really the only logical place for us to begin this journey together.

As we sat in his study and Bill talked about how he created his successes in life and business, it became crystal clear of what I should call these concepts and the reasons why.

Exercise: *Stop right now!* Before you go any further, I am giving you *complete permission* to write in this book. Underline stuff, highlight (with multiple colors) concepts you find important to you and mark up this book in any way you feel led to do. Remember when I mentioned in the introduction that this book isn't *just* to be read? *Well, I was serious!* If you don't have a pen or some crayons in hand, stop right now and go get them! I'm serious about sharing this stuff; are you committed to learning it?

 POWER THOUGHT: Success begins when you decide to make it personal.

Exercise: Get yourself a notebook and write down action steps you can take to get faster results. Treat this like a real course you are studying in school. Don't allow yourself to be passive. Instead, choose a passionate attitude and your results will arrive much faster. For those who are really serious, you will see that later in the book I will talk about a special planner and organization system that I use to achieve my goals in record time. If you would like to use the same system that I do, you can pick up one of these planners on my website **www.DouglasVermeeren.com.** They are not an expensive tool and are worth the investment if you really want to fast-track your learning and progress.

The title, which you have already seen, is *Personal Power Mastery,* or PPM for short.

Here's the **why,** and when you truly understand and own this concept, you will already have gone a long way toward creating more prosperity and abundance in your life.

Personal: Your journey to success must become personal. It is not something that can be delegated or entrusted to another. **Your life is yours to live.** You cannot give any responsibility for the life you wish to create to another. As we say in our seminars, **"If you own it, you can change it."** Until you take full responsibility for everything in your life, you cannot expect to improve on it.

Your success is a result of your decision to be powerful on a personal level.

Exercise: Your first commitment will be to recognize that you are personally responsible for the results you desire. *Make that commitment now!* Record your thoughts in your progress journal on why it is really up to you personally to assume responsibility for your outcomes.

Power: Power represents the ability to act, which is the foundational concept in creating success. Too often, those who are less successful will not acknowledge the power that they have to create new outcomes in their lives. They often accept what life gives them rather than taking action proactively to make things happen. Top achievers move forward and recognize that they have the power to influence outcomes and improve their chances of living their lives by design. **Your actions are the foundation of your power.**

Exercise: Your second major commitment is to recognize that you *can* take action. Your movements can rearrange everything. As you will soon learn, major active shifts are not always required to make progress. *You have the power within you.* Consider what power you have used to create positive results in the past and also where you *could* have taken action in the past but *chose* not to.

Mastery: Mastery is a term that represents a process. Mastery does not occur instantly, yet is a state that can be created through effort, practice and constant improvement. I am reminded of a conversation that Pablo Picasso, the famous painter, once had. Someone called him a master, and his response was, "If you knew how hard I worked to get to where I am you would not call me a master at all." All individuals that have achieved mastery will very quickly share that it was a process. Think of it as a journey rather than a destination. The idea of mastery should also give hope to you, no matter where you are currently in pursuit of your dreams. *Every master was once a disaster.*

One of my hobbies is training and competing in martial arts. I specifically train in Brazilian Jiu-Jitsu, where the body and mind are both challenged. Martial arts, in general, provide many important lessons that are applicable to real life. Through this book, I will be sharing these essential lessons I have learned about success. Many of these teachings will serve as powerful confirmation of the PPM lessons.

Lesson: When I first started Brazilian Jiu-Jitsu, I quickly realized I didn't know very much at all. My goal quickly shifted from winning to simply finding a way to survive. It didn't take me long to realize if I analyzed what had happened when I lost a match I would gain insight that would protect me from making a similar mistake in the next round.

Slowly, I began to add to my skill level drop by drop until I was able to shift from being a completely defensive player to controlling many of the outcomes in my favor. These results shifted simply because I was committed to showing up and putting in the hard work. Mastery is not instant but progress can be. Mastery is the result of consistency. **Each lesson in failure moves you one step closer to mastery.**

Exercise: Mastery requires consistent application and learning of these principles. Schedule a 10- to 20-minute block of time each day to learn and develop a plan for implementation. Progress will be a result of consistent effort.

Each of these elements is a step in a progression toward creating more success. Personal responsibility proceeds the power of action. The power of action proceeds progress toward mastery. **You have the power to create new consequences.**

One of the most powerful realizations people experience when they learn about these ideas is that they have the power to create new consequences and results. No matter what your current situation in life is, *you do not have to accept it*. **You can change it**. You can create what you want and what you desire.

Nothing that you have experienced thus far is permanent and most changes can occur quite quickly. The word consequence originates from a French word meaning sequel, or that which follows. I like the idea of a sequel. While the past has some bearing on the story, it is not *the end* of the story. There are multiple scenes and chapters just waiting to be discovered!

You too have a history. Although past discouragement and lack might be part of your life's current feature, *anything can happen in your sequel*. Your consequences haven't yet been finalized.

The good news is that some stories can have some dramatic shifts from tragedy to extreme victory. Perhaps that will be your new adventure?

POWER THOUGHT: Events by themselves have very little power until we give them meaning or significance. Don't let negative reactions create a negative circumstance.

Jack is one of my students in Las Vegas. When he arrived on our doorstep, he had experienced several significant and heartbreaking challenges. Although he had good intentions, he had created failing patterns in his life. As I have observed, most people stay the same because their patterns are also just as predictable. These patterns manifested themselves in his employment history, in his relationships, and in his personal health care. As he arrived, he was bitter and filled with blame toward others for his circumstances.

Without accepting the "personal" involvement in his life in the past, he was not able to own the results he was experiencing. As he believed that his current situations were a result of circumstances beyond his control, he had no motivation to take any actions to change his situation. Mastery was not a possible outcome in this state, and his patterns were destined to repeat themselves again and again. For Jack, life became a state of default rather than choice.

When Jack arrived, he had gained a significant amount of weight. His fast food budget was approximately $300 per week. His mother's significant relationship had ended in a bitter divorce, and his other family relationships were strained. At work, his efforts were recognized as substandard and met minimum requirements. Jack's attitude of "what is meant to be will be" caused him to take a less than proactive approach. He was unsatisfied and worried.

It was a final stern warning to "pull up his socks or move on" from his supervisor that brought enough pain where he decided he needed rescuing.

When Jack arrived on our steps, he was desperate. That desperation turned into hope when he realized the concepts of PPM.

He accepted his personal responsibility in changing his life and circumstances.

He owned his power to act and shifted from reacting to being proactive.

He committed to a process of mastery even though it was often uncomfortable.

Within a short period of time, he began to see new outcomes that were more favorable. The more his situation began to improve, the further he recognized his ability to possess PPM. This realization was the beginning of change for Jack, and it will be for anyone who makes an attempt.

 POWER THOUGHT: If you push yourself to create better patterns that cause you to grow and stretch, your patterns can be a source of power.

This realization led to Jack changing many of the patterns he had experienced over and over again in his life. As he gained mastery, he began to cultivate greater feelings of self-worth and power. (Remember, our definition is the ability to act.) This growth in power started to create new and improved consequences that, up until this point, Jack had only dreamed about.

Instead of fearing the conclusion of his job, he soon earned a raise. He shifted his eating habits and began to improve his health and physical appearance. Due to the recognition that he had control over how he interacted with the people in his life, Jack began to improve his relationships. Soon he found the woman he also now calls the love of his universe. Everything in Jack's life became effortless and success followed. Jack maintains these outcomes through his ownership of personal power and his ongoing quest to *master it all.* You can do the same.

Again, regardless of where you begin, the consequence or sequel remains yet to be. What content will you create?

The Path to Increased Happiness

As I interviewed the top achievers, along with those who were less successful, I made an interesting discovery. Happiness and feelings of self-worth and contentment are not attached to a specific level of accomplishment, or even to the accumulation of a certain number of units of money, cars, clothing, houses, vacations or awards. Happiness is, in fact, most attached to *constant* progress.

When people feel as though they are progressing, they experience greater happiness. This is the journey toward mastery that we are referring to.

Nicole had just lost her husband in military action in the Middle East. She was lost, confused and struggled with depression. She moved back to her parents' home and brought her two toddlers with her. The more she thought about her dire situation, the more Nicole slumped further into a feeling of hopelessness and powerlessness.

Each day seemed to drag Nicole further down, and the answers on how to cope and raise her children seemed to get even cloudier. One day, while surfing the internet, Nicole caught one of the weekly YouTube episodes that I share on the strength of the PPM program. As fate would have it, the topic I was discussing was the idea of finding happiness through progress.

Following that episode, Nicole wrote to me and reported that it was quite a struggle to believe that the PPM principles could help her. That was until a small voice inside of her, which she felt came from her late husband, whispered that it was time for her to get up and start doing something. So she decided to put these concepts to the test.

POWER THOUGHT: You must be willing to let go of where you are to get to where you are going. Don't let past frustrations keep you from future victories.

The progress was slow at first (the truth is that results will come to you as quickly as you decide you are ready to receive them). The results did begin to arrive for Nicole, and changes started happening. She could see progress and positive changes in her life, which brought on happier feelings. Soon, Nicole and her children were out in the world again. However, things did not stop there. She discovered a powerful key that many families who have lost someone in combat need to hear. Nicole made a conscious decision to start speaking about what she learned. She initially reached out to church groups and then with other assemblies that would welcome her.

The last time I checked in with Nicole, she had decided to write a book with a vision to help others who were going through the same experiences she had faced. Nicole realized she had different choices to make and ran with them. Now, she is impacting lives because of what she learned and opened herself up to.

It wasn't until she really started making progress with purpose that her life began to feel happy again. However, she confessed that her greatest joy came when she began to see how she could help others around her.

Think about this: (and we'll talk about this more in the final chapters of this book) your happiness will increase exponentially as you share and develop these principles in others.

Happiness comes from sharing our progress and using our progress to bless the lives of others in addition to our own.

As you proceed through each of the upcoming chapters, please keep these three important elements in mind as you complete the exercises. I will put a brief reminder at the head of each chapter to follow.

As I mentioned at the beginning of the chapter, it was during the conversation with Bill that I realized that every top achiever I had studied up until that point recognized the importance of these three elements. All top achievers were personally invested in their future, recognized their capacity or power to act, and sought out constant improvement in the journey to mastery. You will achieve it in the same way.

Comfort Zone Versus Brilliance Zone

As we embark on this journey, there is another principle that is crucial to discuss: the concept of comfort zones. Many self-help gurus today rant and rave about the essential importance of stepping outside of your comfort zone to create success. They are only partially correct.

As I studied and observed the top achievers in multiple industries, I gained some interesting insights into this concept that no one talks about.

In his landmark book *Outliers*, Malcolm Gladwell pointed out that **to become an expert in any given thing often requires more than 10,000 hours**. Top achievers understand the value of effort and time. They don't try to step out of their comfort zone to do everything. In fact, they select where they will be uncomfortable.

 POWER THOUGHT: Top achievers are improvisers, not perfectionists. If you want to create more success in your life, you have to move forward not knowing all the answers.

Napoleon Hill and others pointed out correctly that the riches are in the niches. Find your expertise and then go deep, not wide, into those areas.

One definition of success is to achieve a high level of expertise in a subject area. If you are trying to step out of your comfort zone in all areas, you will never develop depth. As I observed the top achievers around the world, they were not dabblers. They were focused. When they chose to be uncomfortable, it was within specific areas of their brilliance.

When we talk about comfort zones, we encourage our students to shift *first* into their brilliance zone and then *explore* becoming uncomfortable. In other words, focus on your strengths and the areas that are most valuable to you and then step out of your comfort zone to grow those specific areas.

Tara came to one of our events completely burned out. She was trying to start a new business as a single mom. Her energy was stretched and almost sapped dry. She had been following the conventional thought of reaching outside of her comfort zone to learn all the skills she thought she needed for her business to complete all of the things that she thought her new business demanded of her.

When we met Tara, it was clear that she had a very specific set of skills that drew her to the idea of launching her business. These were the abilities that everyone was excited to hire her for. The challenge was that Tara was spending too much time trying to master things outside of her passion and purpose (her "comfort zone"), which was literally pulling herself away from the real reason she started the business, and why people were drawn to her.

Once she grasped this idea of working within her brilliance zone and striving to push her comfort zone there, she began to thrive. Furthermore, she took control of her PPM and began to soar to new heights.

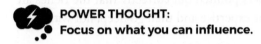

POWER THOUGHT:
Focus on what you can influence.

What About You?

There are a lot of things I can share about you just from your purchase of this book. I know these things about you because they are also true for the people that attend our seminars. You bought this book because of a desire to achieve two outcomes.

The first reason is that individuals are looking for tools or strategies to improve themselves. They want to learn how to become more successful and achieve more.

The second is that people want to learn how to improve their situations. Often this involves learning to increase abundance in order to receive and enjoy a better situation.

Both of these things are related. **To have more, you must become more.**

Rose was a retired schoolteacher. She had been retired for more than two decades, in fact. Most people at her age justify slowing everything down. It's not typically the time in life when people think that their most exciting moments or biggest opportunities are ahead of them.

Rose was determined to learn and grow. She arrived already recognizing that most of the important moments in her life were created when she took personal responsibility for her life, took action, and worked on continuously improving her situation. What she did lack was the timeline that many of her younger classmates in the group had.

She needed results right the first time. She also needed them to appear sooner rather than later. PPM gave her the tools to accelerate her learning and her outcomes. As she became more, she also experienced more. You can enjoy these results too! You are never too old, and it is never too late to make changes that can improve your life. **If you are breathing, you are a perfect candidate for improvement.**

Make a commitment right now that you will expand who you are. This commitment will open the door to possibilities and new consequences.

Exercise: How do you envision your new and improved self? Describe it. Which of the attributes that you admire do you already possess to some degree?

Specific and Clear Equals Attainable and Near

Too often, when I ask someone what he/she really wants out of life, I am given a vague answer that was often borrowed from somewhere else. If they say they want more time, they don't exactly have a number in mind. If people say they want more money, they don't have a specific amount in their heads. If they say they want their company to do better this year, business owners often don't know what areas they want to improve. One of my heroes, Thomas S. Monson, spoke it best when he said, "When we deal in generalities, we shall never succeed. When we deal with specifics, we shall rarely have a failure."

Nathan used this principle to help himself and his family achieve financial freedom and abundance. At our PPM live sessions, there is a question I like to ask our attendees about their financial freedom. I ask the participants to describe it.

Most people come up with vague emotion-driven experiences like having more time off, not having to worry about bills or debt, etc.

Some even describe nice houses, cars or vacations. While these aren't necessarily wrong, what they reported are not expressions of true financial freedom.

Financial freedom is a specific number. It is calculated by determining precisely what your monthly financial obligations are and then understanding how to build a passive income stream that will satisfy that exact amount. When you have done that, you are, by definition, financially free.

With that explanation, Nathan was able to understand exactly where he was in the present. He was then able to understand exactly what he needed to accomplish. Then, he constructed a concrete, specific set of activities that allowed him to achieve the specific number that represented his financial freedom. Up until that point, it was simply a hopeful expression of a wish, want and dream that had no tangible basis in reality.

 POWER THOUGHT: Amazing things cannot be created in the future or the past. You need to use the present.

I encourage many of our students when it comes to vision boards and goals to get very specific and include as many details about the items they want. Write the exact pricing and commitments required to attain those desired items. Include as many specifics and detailed information as you can, and you'll see that those dreams instantly become much closer to real-world reality (more on this later).

Exercise: Get very clear and specific in this exercise. If one of your goals is in direct correlation to your current situation and your level of income, I encourage you to be very explicit about what that amount is or what that lifestyle looks like. We will return to these specifics later in the book and explore some easily accessible systems to create this for you. For now, though, focus on describing it with particulars. Remember: A goal that is specific and clear becomes attainable and near.

I want to conclude this chapter with one last story that I am proud of. Naturally, these principles work for everyone, but my favorite success stories reflect those who start in youth. One of my students is a young girl named Tegan. At the time of writing this book, she is nine years old.

Using the principles of PPM, Tegan is growing her career as a motivational speaker and author. She has three best-selling books on Amazon and has shared the stage with some of the biggest names in the speaking business. In fact, recently she spoke at an event hosted by my friend John Demartini, from the movie *The Secret*, and me, in London. We have many more plans for this young superstar. Who knows – perhaps you'll even see her on stage at one of my events you attend.

Using the principles, you are about to experience how she has been able to open doors of opportunity and unlock possibilities for her future that some adults will only dream about.

You Are Awesome!

Before we venture forward, I want to remind you of something that I think we all too often forget about ourselves. You are *awesome*. You really are. I'm not just saying that. I've thought long and hard about this point.

We are going to talk more about what makes you so awesome. There really is so much more to you than you realize.

I love what my friend Alex Mandossian says, "You're not as good as you think you are. You're better." It is a profound truth that most people don't think enough of themselves. Now obviously I'm not suggesting you get a puffed-up ego about your sense of self, but I am inviting you to get a true sense of your self-worth.

That is not an ego issue. It is a reality check.

Too often, people fail to succeed because they feel they are not worth it or that they need to qualify for greatness. **You already have everything you need**. Trust me about that. I've spent time with the most elite achievers in the world, and I've spent time with people at the other end of the spectrum. I've even seen people at the far end of the spectrum turn things around and arrive at the highest levels of success.

In fact, one of the top achievers I spent time with started on welfare and became the 25th wealthiest man in the United States. Maybe you've heard of him, Bill Bartmann. If you haven't heard of Bill, look him up. He was an incredible individual.

The point I want to stress here is that you *can* do it. You can really create the life you desire. Your timing is perfect.

As my friend Randy Gage once told me, "We are living in the best time in the history of the world. It has never been easier to create wealth, abundance and opportunity."

There never has been, nor ever will be, another you. You are unique, and you have special gifts to share. You have a powerful legacy that is only yours to create. **This is your time!**

Your time here on this planet is short and flies by so quickly. What will you do with your time? What will you create? What will you leave behind?

Let's get cracking! Don't delay. Head straight to the next chapter to access the force that is *Personal Power Mastery*!

 **POWER THOUGHT:**
Live by design. Create with purpose.

Power Mastery Questions to Consider:

1. How are you currently involved in your own success personally?

2. What activities are you engaged in that demonstrate your power?

3. How are you building your mastery each day?

4. When have you scheduled your improvement each day?

5. What areas of strength do you already possess?

6. How can progress / increase your happiness?

7. How can helping others increase your happiness?

8. Who can you help today?

9. How can you become more specific and clear about what you want in life?

10. Consider how unique you are among all of the creations in the universe.

11. What are some of the gifts you have that no one else does?

12. Are you ready to get started?

CHAPTER TWO

The Power of Choice

Destiny is not a matter of chance
but a matter of choice.

William Jennings Bryan

**You have the personal responsibility
to make your own choices**

You have the power to act on your personal choices

**You will develop the ability to master making
better choices as you make them**

This first step of choice is often the most difficult for people to grasp, especially if they have convinced themselves that they are on the receiving end of what the world is doing to them. It is challenging for men and women to understand that they *do* have a choice. They don't have to accept their reality as it currently arrives.

Individuals really struggle with the concept that they *can* make a choice about what they experience. As a result, they settle for life as it appears rather than make active choices to create new possibilities. Choice is your first and greatest power.

If you want to create better outcomes in your life, you have to really believe that you can make choices. Your decisions make a difference.

It is a very easy thing to say, but… do you really believe it?

Even those who are in the most problematic circumstances can make choices that will affect their futures.

Remember, choice is a principle of freedom. If you recognize that you are free to choose, you must accept that you also have the freedom to create new outcomes.

Choice is your **first power**. Choice is also your **greatest power**. If you are receiving negative consequences that differ from what you envision for your life, hear this: you have a choice. It doesn't matter whether these consequences stem from things you are presently doing or something that was done to you. You don't have to keep it in your life.

It has broken my heart to hear what some of the people in my seminars have been through. I have heard first-hand stories of abuse (sexual, physical, verbal and mental). I have heard about situations of bullying, not just among teenagers and school kids, but also among adults who work together. I have heard of people in deep depression to the point of suicidal thoughts and despair. However, even those in these situations have still held intact the power of choice.

If this is the situation you are currently in, please start by knowing that I genuinely feel compassion for you. My heart sorrows for what you must be going through. But there is hope and you do have choices. In the power of choice, you will find freedom and healing. We will speak later about how to receive needed support to make empowering choices that will allow you to put these hurtful things behind you.

It is very easy to forget the possibility of choice if you have suffered certain experiences over a long period of time.

Even those who are not at the most tragic end of the spectrum forget that they have a choice. It is not uncommon to have people attend our events to share that they feel like the time is past for them to improve their performance at work, improve their situation at home or in a relationship, or to pursue an entrepreneurial idea they are drawn to. They deny the power of choice.

It's almost as if they feel like they are on a TV game show and they've just locked in their final answer for everything to come.

 POWER THOUGHT: Choice is the first power toward creating new outcomes. If you want a new situation, start today by making different choices.

Recently I spoke at a maximum security prison in North Carolina. This was one of the most intimidating scenarios I have ever experienced. The point worth noticing, however, was that even the inmates in their cells *still* possessed the ability to make choices. It doesn't matter where you are; options are always available to you!

Darin was a murderer. As he explained what he had done, I genuinely believed him when he said he really didn't mean for it to happen. "Things just got out of control," Darin stated and shook his head. "I don't really even know how it happened."

An argument between himself and another teenage boy named Tavin escalated to a point where a gun was drawn. Wringing his hands in front of him, Darin revealed that the thing that upset him the most was that there was a time when he was friends with Tavin. Darin was at Tavin's birthday party when he was seven.

"It never should have happened and I'm sorry." Darin looked up at me and smiled. "I was angry at the time. I was angry when I got here. I blamed everyone and everything. But since then I made a choice. I decided to stop being angry. I decided to stop blaming others for my actions. That choice has made it possible for me to look outside myself. I may be here in prison, but a kid I knew lost his life, and all for a stupid argument. I'm sorry for what happened. He was my friend back in the day."

His choice to sincerely own what happened allowed the healing process to begin. Although Darin can never erase the consequences of his previous choices, he has the power to decide how he will proceed from here.

C.S. Lewis once said, "You can't go back and change the beginning, but you can start where you are and change the ending." That change starts with the power of choice.

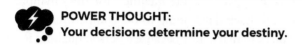

POWER THOUGHT:
Your decisions determine your destiny.

We will talk later about the concept of judgment and decision making, but for now, let's spend some time on the ability to choose.

No matter what circumstance you find yourself in, choice is the one power that can never be taken from you. We don't ever have to accept the conditions or situations we find ourselves in. We don't have to believe and receive the attitudes and interpretations we have over the situations we are currently experiencing.

Very often, it is easy to look at all of the negative situations and think, *Those guys sure do need this pep talk on choice, but I'm pretty successful! I don't need to think about it as much.*

One of my best friends is an Olympian named Jason Parker. Jason had achieved high levels of competitive success as a speed skater. He had competed in multiple competitions around the world as a high-level athlete. He fought hard to compete at an Olympic level, but for some reason, didn't qualify.

He tried again and missed his time by fractions of a second! In fact, Jason had to watch from a distance on television as people he had beaten previously took his place in the Olympic competition.

Let's reflect on this.

Jason had a choice to make. He was getting older and the competition was only getting more intense and fierce. Training at this level was not only rough on his body but required massive commitments of time, effort, energy and money.

He had already accomplished so much. There really wasn't a need to prove himself to anyone. Yet, he made a choice. His dream was to compete in the Olympics and this goal led him to give it another try.

He gave it his all, and it paid off. He qualified for the Olympic Games in Torino, Italy. Each day leading to the competition there were additional choices to make. Just because a person qualifies for the Olympics does not mean that they have the luxury of slowing down. In fact, he chose to turn up the volume on everything. In the end, it paid off, and he became an Olympian medalist.

 POWER THOUGHT: Success is living your life by decision. You're where you want to be, doing the things that excite you, inspire you and bring out the best in you and those around you.

Choice Requires Alternatives

When there is only one choice, there is *no* choice. Choice requires options and there are always various ones to choose from. No matter how positive or negative your situation may appear, you have options. Alternatives may come across as limited, but the bottom line is – they are still there.

Those opportunities may not always be in opposition to each other. Truthfully, some of your options may only be slight variations of a similar path. However, even those small details still allow for a choice.

One of the greatest strengths you can develop is to see choice when most people would think there isn't any.

Exercise: In your journal, take a situation you have been struggling with and brainstorm some possible choices you may consider. While you don't necessarily have to pursue any of the choices you identify, there is power in developing the skill to recognize alternatives.

Recognizing options is a skill and a talent that very few people develop. One of the most powerful activities for students of PPM is encouraging our students to journal each day about difficult choices they are facing and the options available to them. In other words, every day I spur these students on to take a difficult issue in their lives and brainstorm several different options around choices that could be made regarding that issue. Naturally, they develop several new and often beneficial approaches to something that otherwise felt hopeless. In addition, they change their thinking to be *possibility-minded* rather than *problem-focused*. Try it.

Choice is Selecting

As you have expressed a desire to make your life better by purchasing this book, it is essential that I point out that choice is actually the act of selecting. You are taking a step of action. When you make a choice, you are selecting outcomes and possibilities. As part of this process, you are denying or excluding consequences.

In other words, **choosing is actually saying either yes or no to possibilities in your future**. This is the first step to creating your life by design. The moment you realize you have this power, it sets the stage for reshaping the way things currently are. **You can have any future you pick.**

You can't not make a choice. We can learn from successful people and from those who are not as successful. I learned a valuable insight on choice from a homeless man I met on a park bench in France. As we engaged in conversation, we began to talk about the power of choice. He confessed to me that making a choice for him was too hard. Most of the time he felt his choices didn't matter and there was no point in worrying about it. He felt that most of the time making choices was too risky and often a gamble. It was too easy to make a wrong choice, so it was often simpler to sit back and not take any action. This man also stated that he didn't have the power to change much. "What differences do my choices make in the end?" he questioned. The answer is clear and straightforward: what was going to occur was destined to take shape, whether he did anything about it or not.

Certainly, this point of view is in direct opposition to the concepts of PPM.

By giving up the power of choice, he surrendered his outcomes to forces outside of his control. In his particular circumstances, the result was terrible.

 POWER THOUGHT: There is a difference between "can't" and "won't." Some people have decided they "can't" be successful when the truth is they have actually decided they "won't."

Choice is a Form of Control

When you recognize that you have choices, you regain control of situations that might otherwise leave you with a sense of loss. Evaluating the choices in a situation beforehand can restore hope from moments of hopelessness.

Feeling that you have this power of choice can give you strength in difficult times and give you hope for the future.

I am often in awe when I see people in our seminars really grasp the **power of choice**. When people understand how much power they really have in their lives to choose, big things begin to happen. **You can never overdevelop this power.**

Usually, when I encounter those who feel that life is unfair or out of control, it is important to remind them of this power of choice. Choice puts you back in the driver's seat.

The next time you're feeling helpless or hopeless, pause for a moment. Identify what choices are currently within your power, and you see control and power return back into your hands.

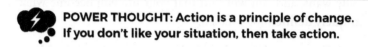 **POWER THOUGHT: Action is a principle of change. If you don't like your situation, then take action.**

Now is a good time to remind you of the first word in our program's name: *Personal.* For choice to really become a powerful force in your life, **you must personally get involved in considering and making the choices for your own life.** If you delegate these to others by following what the masses move forward with, or by choosing to simply follow the program, you are not taking personal responsibility.

No one will make good choices on your behalf. For the most part, everyone is trying to improve their situation. Your best future is not on their radar. If you want significant improvement in your life, then you will have to make that choice personally.

The Other Meaning of Choice

There is another meaning of choice that we don't often consider. Trust me, though, and look in a dictionary. There you will find this other definition. Choice is an expression used to describe a certain quality. For example, you may choose to eat the choicest fruits and vegetables, meaning those that are of the highest quality.

When you are making your choices or selections, make sure that you are choosing the highest quality options available to you. We will talk more about this in decision making but, for now, understand that all choices have lasting consequences. **By choosing the highest quality of choices, you will be receiving the highest quality of life.**

When you make specific choices, you will get specific results. If you simply say I want to have a better life, you will find that the choices you make from that point of view won't improve a thing. Make a commitment to a **specific** choice that resonates with what you really want, and you will find that your life will become what you **uniquely defined** for yourself.

Exercise: Once you have identified some options you wish to consider as choices, think through the possible consequences that may follow. Some choices that appear simple or straightforward may be flawed and may not provide for the outcomes that you truly desire.

As I studied the top achievers and those who were less successful, I noticed some substantial differences in the way these two groups used their powers of choice. We will spend quite a bit of time on this in future chapters to get into the really important differences, but two of the ones I want to mention at this stage are that the more successful achievers very often recognized that they had a choice; the less successful individuals gave up their ability to choose more often. They simply submitted to suggestions or ideas of others and, as a result, often felt helpless.

The other enormous difference was that the most successful achievers did not rush into making a decision without considering the long-term results that would form by making this particular choice. With the more important issues in front of them, they slowed down the process to *really* understand alternatives. In some cases, they would even get advice from a trusted advisor or mentor.

 POWER THOUGHT: If you are serious about your success, you need to seek out the best in everything to help you get there.

Intuition

The more essential the choice, the more the heart plays a factor in consideration. We will talk later about emotions, feelings and values. Because many of these concepts do overlap, it is crucial to point out that the more important a choice is, the more likely it is that the answers are going to be felt rather than found.

Your **intuition will serve you well** in many circumstances. I have personally found when I trust my heart on some choices, even when I have made an error, I am confident with my decision because it felt like the right thing to do.

It is not fair for me to give you my definition of success because that is something you must determine for yourself. I will say this about success, though. After having personally met with and interviewed first-hand many of the world's top achievers, success isn't money, power, material goods, or any of that stuff. **Success is being happy about the choices you have made.**

 POWER THOUGHT: Lasting change always begins with a vision of a better, positive and compelling future.

The choice I'd like to invite you to make right now is to keep reading.

Questions About Choice to Consider:

1. What does it mean to take personal accountability for your choices?

2. What does it mean to assume the power to act when making choices?

3. How can you increase your mastery of making choices?

4. What choices are you currently facing?

5. What options do you have?

6. Are you choosing the best options?

7. Are there trusted advisors you can share some of your choices with?

8. Are there trusted advisors you ask to help you explore your choice options?

9. How do you feel about choices you are currently making?

10. What can you do if you feel a loss of control?

CHAPTER THREE

The Power of Thought

Thinking is becoming.
Therefore, be extremely careful
in your thinking.

Sri Chinmoy

**You have the personal responsibility
to make your own thoughts**

**You have the power or the ability
to act on your personal thoughts**

**You will develop the ability
to master choosing better thoughts**

Thoughts become things. You've heard this before. Most people understand the concept. However, the majority of people don't understand how your thoughts can become things and how to control the thoughts that ultimately become this reality.

Very early in my research of the world's top achievers and in my comparisons with those who were less successful, it became very apparent that all people had thoughts and aspirations to bring good things into their lives. Having "good" thoughts, however, is not enough.

In fact, good thoughts aren't even the best expression of the kinds of thoughts you are going to need if you really want positive results in your life.

There are several research articles I had read over the years that provide estimates of how many thoughts we have as individuals each day. Reports from the National Science Foundation place the estimate between 12,000 to 60,000 thoughts. There are other studies that suggest the numbers are as high as 70,000 to 80,000 thoughts in a day! That's a lot of thinking!

Quality of Thought

While quantifying the number of thoughts we have is interesting, the real value comes when we analyze the **quality of those thoughts** and what it really takes to create reality from them.

The thoughts that create our real-world scenarios follow two patterns.

The first pattern centers on the frequency of these thoughts. There are many popular quotes and sayings that reaffirm the idea that what you think about most often influences you most. This is certainly true, and I support it.

While the frequency is significant, the quality of those thoughts is critical as well. One consideration that is rarely cited when pointing out the idea of 12,000, 60,000 or even 80,000 thoughts a day is that, for the average person, more than 70-80% of those thoughts are what is known as negative or neutral thinking.

 POWER THOUGHT: We act on what we reflect on most. (both positive and negative)

Most people have heard about negative thinking. A lot have heard about positive thinking. Many individuals have never heard of neutral thinking. There is one more type of thinking that most people haven't heard about either. Let's talk about all the kinds of thinking here so you can make some choices and recognize which kind is going to support you most in your efforts at creating outcomes that are more successful.

One of the best ways to teach this is to think about water and the principle of buoyancy. Buoyancy is the ability that something has to float in water. If something is negatively buoyant, it sinks. If something is positively buoyant, it floats to the surface. If something is neutrally buoyant, it neither sinks nor floats. A swimming fish is a good example.

Using this analogy can be a great way to understand the power and quality of thoughts.

Negative thinking: Like things that are negatively buoyant, negative thoughts sink right to the bottom. They lead to as low as you can go. **There is no power here.** There is also very little hope. Thankfully, most people do not spend all of their time in negative thinking, but the more time you spend here, the more depressing life becomes. In truth, most people who create situations of depression in their lives do so because they spend significant amounts of time in the abyss of negative thinking. In most cases (apart from certain medical conditions), **spending time here is a choice.** Negative thinking is also paralyzing. In the past, you've probably noticed that if you became frustrated or someone said something that irritated you, it was very hard to be productive in this state. **Negative thinking never produces positive outcomes.** Quite the opposite, in fact.

Neutral thinking: This type is not talked about a lot. In reality, this one is important to understand because it is where most people spend most of their time. It is the kind of thinking that we don't really choose. We just let it happen. Sometimes it's called **autopilot.** In the psychology field, I have seen the activities that accompany this kind of thinking called **ritual tendencies.** These are the things that we just do without really thinking about. They become as familiar as brushing our teeth or putting on our socks and shoes.

The challenge with this kind of thinking is that since it isn't really creating any frustration or pain, we simply let it slide. However, it is the one level that often robs us of becoming greater, more so than negative thinking. You see, by doing nothing or just going with the flow, we maintain the average. We will miss so much if we allow ourselves to remain here.

 POWER THOUGHT: Extraordinary results rarely appear from those engaged in average actions.

In addition, neutral thinking is never just neutral in the long term. Let's jump back into the water for a minute. What eventually happens with all things that start out as neutrally buoyant over time? Well, they become negatively buoyant and they sink. The same is true of neutral thinking. If you stay in the same neutral thinking for a long enough time, you'll become frustrated and disillusioned because you aren't making progress; then those thoughts eventually lead closer and closer to the bottom. At some point, even a neutral person gets stuck in the mud of despair along with the seaweed at the bottom of the ocean. Ask yourself, is that where you *really* want to be?

Consider the last time you saw someone feel overly excited about dedicating their life to watching TV, playing video games and eating potato chips. Eventually, they will feel depressed, which robs them of their ambition to create big things.

Positive thinking: This is the next level up, but it is certainly not the highest. I feel like positive thinking has been very misunderstood over the years. I believe that most people who throw the idea around have confused it with the next and highest level of thinking. They don't know any better, so they accept it as it is. Now, I know what I am about to reveal here may surprise some, and some might even outright disagree with me.

Victim Mentality

Positive thinking is a form of victim mentality.

Yes, I said it, and I'm going to *prove* it. Let's go back to the water analogy. I keep using this image because it is so powerful and compelling. Positive buoyancy is at the top of the water, but it is still in the water. That means that even something floating on the water allows itself to be influenced, but by the water it floats on and is surrounded by.

This is exactly what we see with so-called positive thinkers. They need elements in their environment to respond to. In other words, they are victim thinkers because they need an emergency to respond to. If they don't have a plight, they create one instead.

Let's take a closer look. Positive thinkers always look on the bright side of what's not working. For example, they say, "I missed my bus. Well, look on the positive side of things: the next bus may have a person I'm supposed to meet on it." Or, "I lost my job, but that's okay. I can go now and start the business I've been meaning to." Here is another scenario: "My spouse is divorcing me, but that'll be for the best because there is probably someone else who is meant to love me."

It's all still *reactive* thinking. Not *proactive*. It is responsive to the situation around them. This is not the type of thinking that top achievers participate in.

So what is the top kind of thinking? Are you holding on to your hats?

It is called **empowered** or **proactive thinking**. This level is the first one that is actually out of the water because it does not allow the situations around itself to control how it is thinking or responding. This kind of thinking chooses independence of outside sources on how it will proceed and what it will decide upon.

 POWER THOUGHT: If you are *proactive* in life, your ability to make more choices increases. If you are *reactive* in life, your ability to make more choices decreases.

If you are going to create a life with purpose, you need to rise to this kind of thinking. I am not saying it is always easy; it means you will really have to pay attention in the next two chapters. You will have to buckle down and understand the power of change and values in your life. We will get to that soon enough. For now, let's share some more ideas around thought.

Emotions Come From Thinking

How you think about a situation ultimately dictates how you will feel about it. How you choose to process a situation will determine how you feel about it. Those feelings will either create positive or negative energy. Emotions paint your reality, so it is very important to recognize that your evaluation of situations is not always a correct assessment.

Allow me to stress this here: bad days are often a choice. What really ruined your day wasn't the situation; rather, it was your *interpretations* of it. If you want to be a truly successful person, you need to practice the Buddhist idea of separation. **You are not the event and the event is not you.**

You must be proactive as the event arrives and learn to control your emotions through situations that may not feel favorable. This is much harder to do than it sounds, and I totally get that. It is, in fact, impossible for humans to *completely* detach themselves from emotion, and they shouldn't. However, as I observed the top 400 achievers, I found that they had a powerful skill of rebounding from negative situations quickly without letting it affect their emotions long term. They recognized they had power in their ability to respond. Yes, power is brought up here again. How quickly you are able to cope with the difficulty or improve the situation rather than react often makes all the difference in the world.

 POWER THOUGHT: Events by themselves have very little power until we give them meaning or significance. Don't let negative reactions create negative circumstances.

In some cases, the less successful people became more paralyzed and didn't respond at all. Generally, this made their situations worse. Sometimes they became angry, hurtful or critical, and that made their situation even worse. If you rewind to the very outset of this book – the idea of success starting with making it *personal* – then you understand why hurtful criticism, anger, bitterness or hate will never help you create success.

Later in the book, we will talk about relating to others, and I will share some strategies that I have observed which work very well for emotive individuals or dealing with others in high emotional states. We create strategies and triggers to activate those strategies when they are needed for the moment they occur. We will talk more about that shortly, and for those who have been to a live session of PPM, you'll remember that this is an important part of that training.

Thoughts Create Beliefs

As I have studied people and the psychology of human behavior and beliefs, it has been interesting to see how our beliefs follow a pattern of development. We encounter an idea, a stimulus or a concept. On its own, that concept is neutral. As we encounter it for the first time, it either finds a place among something we either believe already or do not believe. Obviously, most things arrive in shades of gray, meaning that they are not absolutes. These thoughts become strengthened when they attach themselves to emotions or events that either make them more solid as beliefs, or we discard them as things we do not believe.

Throughout our lives, we will then look for evidence to cling to what we have endorsed or denied as part our of belief structure. You'll notice that I haven't once used the word fact or truth. There are many things we hold as either truth or fact that aren't necessarily so.

The Five Ways Your Mind Learns

As I have studied people and psychology, I have come up with a theory that I call *The 5 Ways Your Mind Learns*. I have found this theory to have many applications from persuasion and influence in sales all the way to interactions in human relationships.

I will explain these five ways and share a little about each one along the way. I believe they are very important if we are to understand thought and improve our thinking. The following are not in any particular order.

1. **Factual learning:** When our mind encounters something presented as a fact or truth, we file it in a certain and particular way. 1 + 1 = 2, the sky is blue, a car has four wheels, and so forth. These are all ideas that we consider undisputed. It is important to note, however, that two people can look at a similar situation and have a different interpretation of facts. When discussing relationships, this may come in handy for you.

2. **Experiential learning:** This kind of learning refers to things that can only be learned through experience. For example, playing a guitar, learning how to ride a bike, playing a sport are all illustrations of something that you can't learn from a book or have someone simply explain it to you. You can only learn this through experience.

3. **Social learning:** There are many things we learn just through associations with the people around us. The family you belong to, the community you live in, the church group you affiliate yourself with, your race, and your social networks. These are all ways in which you've been socially influenced. (It was fascinating to notice that many of the top achievers I spent time with in my research directly correlated their success to surrounding themselves with high-level peers.)

4. **Spatial learning:** Spatial learning has two engaging considerations in how it takes place in the mind. The first is what I call **external spatial learning**. It has to do with how we organize things in relation to each other. For example, if you are hanging a picture, how do you adjust it in relation to the wall so it is hanging straight? Or, perhaps while you are building a jigsaw puzzle, how do you organize the pieces of that puzzle to create the image you see on the box? Perhaps you are playing a game like Tetris or Gummy Drop? These are all exercises in external spatial learning. Spatial learning also occurs inside your mind in a way that is unique. Remember my definition of spatial learning as a form of organization? The way you file information inside your mind is a form of spatial learning.

Here's a fun example. I want you to think of a dog, right now. Picture the dog. How big is that dog? What color? What kind of dog? Please get a really good picture of the dog in your mind. Most likely, you are thinking of a different kind of dog than the one I have imagined. In fact, when we have done this at our live events, we can often have as many different imaginary dogs as there are people in the room. Everyone organizes things somewhat differently in their mind.

This is true of many other words and ideas. When we share this in a sales training setting, it's important that you have a very clear understanding of what the other person is trying to communicate in terms of values, terms, agreements and so forth. (Don't worry, there is a book coming for those who want to learn more about how to use this information in those kinds of settings.)

5. **Intuitional learning:** This one is the most difficult to explain, but it is also one of the most valuable to learn from. It is the *feeling* part of your mind. The best way to describe it is simply **intuition**. It is the feeling that you get when you feel something is correct or incorrect. It is the most important way

you learn. It is also the place I believe most of our regret in life comes from. When you know in your heart that you are called to do something and you don't do it, that's the worst kind of regret you can experience.

Choice of Influences

Thoughts, and the way we process our thoughts, are all things that, for the most part, happen automatically. Be that as it may, there is one thing that we certainly *can* control if we are going to practice empowered thinking or proactive thinking; the kinds of influences we will allow to connect with and shape our thoughts.

We also set the pace for our thoughts deliberately at the beginning of each day. That is the best time to do it, and this is what I observed with the top achievers in my study. All of them did this in fact, not just some of them. They started their day on *their* terms and gave *their* thoughts direction through reading good books, planning their day or reviewing their goals. As emphasized earlier, how you start your day will often dictate the kind of day you will have.

Throughout the day, the top achievers were also careful of the kinds of influences they allowed into their mind. If there was anything out of harmony with what they had set out to think, they were quick to **recognize it** and either **make adjustments** or let their awareness guard against it.

Awareness is Powerful

I have often been surprised and disappointed to hear some gurus advocating the idea of getting rid of all the "toxic" people in your life if you want to be successful. If you think about what we've just learned, that is actually a very immature and reactive approach. It means you are still at the level of letting outside influences control you. If you disassociate from every negative situation or person that comes along you will soon find that you are completely alone.

Let me present a stronger solution (and in fact the one that all top achievers also practice) which will make you aware of toxic or negative things as they appear. You don't have to endorse them as your own feelings or beliefs. Leave them alone or leave them better than when you found them. You will need to be sensitive and wise to know which ones to leave alone. Most situations don't need a solution from you or your involvement.

When you are aware of something negative, also remember that top achievers are not afraid of problems or confrontation. Some issues do need to be dealt with head-on, but how you do so is where you'll find the best answers.

Attitude is a Product of Thought

Attitude is created through long-term exposure to certain thoughts, emotions and beliefs. Attitude paints much of our feelings about what we see. For this chapter, I just want you to understand that your thoughts are the seed from which your attitudes and perceptions are formed.

> *When you defeat the enemy within, no enemy without can harm you.*
>
> **Ancient Samurai saying**

The Control Tower

I want to remind you that you are in control. *You have the ability to choose.* Not only do you have a choice of the thoughts you allow to land and find a place in your mind, but you also get to choose how you feel about those thoughts. The more you can master your mind, the more *power* you will experience. Thoughts lay the groundwork for outcomes.

Thought creates expectations that then become beliefs. Those beliefs are powerful influences on how we will bring forward our efforts in any given situation. I remember as a young kid in grade 1 lining up with all of the kids to run the 100-yard dash. As we left the starting line, it was immediately evident that some of the kids were much faster than others. You could also see the power of belief, as those who believed they were fast enough to push for first place pushed harder. The kids who knew they had fallen behind believed their chances to win were non-existent. They started to slow down and hold back on their best efforts.

Our beliefs influence how much we really try or commit to success. I regularly speak to groups in corporate settings, and I see people at these events who don't really believe in ideas and strategies. They are only willing to give enough effort so that they are not fired. If you don't believe it will work, you won't work. It's as simple as that.

 POWER THOUGHT: You can't wish, want or even think your way to success. At some point, you will have to get to work.

Questions About Thought to Consider:

1. What is negative thinking?

2. What is neutral thinking?

3. What is positive thinking?

4. Why is positive thinking still a victim state?

5. What is empowered thinking?

6. What are the five ways your mind learns?

7. Which ones have influenced you most? Why?

8. How have you been influenced by your experiences?

9. Have they created biases in you?

10. How have you been influenced by those you surround yourself with?

11. Have they created biases in you?

12. Whom would you like to have shaped your thinking?

13. Where will you find them?

14. How are you influenced by spatial learning?

15. How are you influenced by intuitional learning?

16. How are you controlling the influences on your thoughts?

CHAPTER FOUR

The Power of Perception and Belief

What is behind your eyes holds more power than what is in front of them.

- Gary Zukav

You have the power to create your own perceptions

You have the power to change your perceptions

You have the power to better your perceptions

I had just turned five years old, but it is still one of my strongest memories. After kindergarten, my mother picked me up from school and, together with my younger brother, she took us to a magic show. I can still smell the popcorn and cotton candy. As we took our seats and the lights went out, I felt a grand sense of anticipation.

The anticipation turned into wonder as the illusionist took the stage. He brought out a large glass box, threw a golden drape over it, and suddenly it was filled with beautiful ladies in sequin dresses. How could this be possible?

He then took one of the ladies and separated her into a zigzag pattern with her torso far off to one side of the stage, while the rest of her body remained intact on the other. Astonishing!

Next, he took another lady and put her into a trance as she lay across two folding chairs. In this magic state, he was able to remove one of the chairs, and she stayed suspended in the air somehow.

This was what became known as a *hinge day* in my life. A day when something so significant happened that it stirred a passion in me that many of my decisions, loves, priorities, purchases and activities thereafter were permanently shaped by it.

Yes, I began to practice magic and even gave some notable performances. Magic has become a big part of my life and I have enjoyed it ever since. As I conducted my initial success interviews, several world-famous magicians were on the list. Whenever I'm in Las Vegas now, I try to go backstage to connect with the greats like David Copperfield, Penn & Teller, Mack King, Murray Sawchuk,

Nathan Burton and Tommy Wind.

So why do I bring this all up? What do magic tricks and illusions have to do with what I have been bringing up so far? This chapter is about perception, and I can think of **no better illusion than how we perceive the events in our life**. When we observe magic performed by a master, we create a new reality by how we interpret what happens. That is one way to interpret the perception.

For those who know how the illusion is performed, there is a different perspective. Although I know most of the illusions that are implemented by the magicians I watch, my perspective is now affected by how well they perform and execute the illusion. After years of studying magic, I am convinced that this part, the execution and performance, and the connection with the audience is often more important than the mechanics of the illusion itself.

However, there is also a third point of view that I believe is worth sharing, one that makes the illusion work. I think this is what separates the masters from the average magician. You can observe this especially in David Copperfield. The view is that the illusionist, even though he knows how the effect is being performed, still *believes* there is magic. He is a possibility thinker – he can see the invisible and he chooses his perception carefully. That's what really makes the magic on stage possible. This is what really makes people like David Copperfield masters of their craft.

As I have studied the world's top achievers and developed the PPM system, it has become clear to me again and again that the mechanics of the situation are not as important as what those involved choose to believe about it.

 POWER THOUGHT: When you start with you, the outcome changes.

We can learn so much by comparing life to magic. Truly every event or situation we encounter is some form of illusion. There are many ways to interpret the world as we connect with it. This is what I call the *Power of Perception*.

Perception Dictates Possibilities

How we perceive things is very important when considering how success is created. Simply, when we interpret circumstances and events to be supportive, positive, possible and likely, we approach them with a much more powerful level of confidence than when we believe something is challenging, negative or difficult – or even impossible.

Often this definition of perception is compared to the word **belief.** To some degree, this is correct. **Belief has many degrees of commitment and intensity**. When we interact with things in the first experience, they are painted by our beliefs, but they aren't always solidly immovable mantras that dictate our activities. They are more like attitudes toward something. All firm beliefs start this way.

I like to speak of perceptions as a separate power because they are at one end of the belief spectrum. Everything starts with an interpretation that is placed on the continuum of our belief. If we believe and perceive something that backs up that belief, it will grow.

However, as demonstrated by the example of magic and illusions, there are many times in life when our perception creates an incorrect interpretation and, as a result, incorrect assumptions and conclusions are formed. This can be harmful, as our actions are ultimately influenced by what we believe to be true or possible as an outcome.

Consider the last time you believed something that wasn't true. If you're like me, you've had moments where an incorrect belief has cost you opportunities and progress.

You're not the only one. Throughout history, mankind has had beliefs and assumptions that were not correct. Here are a few of the more well-known ones:

The earth is flat.

The earth is the center of the universe.

Here is a funny and bizarre one:

If a car passes 15 mph, the occupants will explode.

On the surface, many of the above beliefs and thoughts may seem ridiculous, but I want to remind you that these published ideas came from some of the greatest thinkers of their time. I guess there is some comfort in knowing that even highly intelligent people get it wrong sometimes.

How about our present day social media accounts and interactions? How many times have we heard, "Well, it must be true because I saw it on Facebook!" Or how about the myriad of opinions on a person's post? Talk about beliefs and perceptions being spewed all over the place!

Now here's something that will help you. You've heard the saying that is often attributed to Henry Ford, **"Whether you think you can or think you can't, you're right."**

This is a powerful concept indeed. If you reflect on this quote, it is basically saying that the event is not as important as your perception or belief surrounding it. The problem or situation is essentially a reactive object that is under the control of the interpretation that is used to describe it. If a thing is considered to be impossible, it will be; if it is thought as an easy thing, it becomes that way.

This leads to the next point about perception, which is the foundation of PPM and brings us back to the idea of choice.

 POWER THOUGHT: Your life is a reflection of what you think it should be. If you think it should be hard, it will be. If you think it should be easy, it will be.

Perception is a Choice

Perception is a matter of choice, and so is perspective. It is easy to say that we all have a choice in how we will interpret ideas and situations we encounter, but life is not that simple.

Let me share an example from my own life.

When I was in the eighth grade, my great-grandmother passed away. This was really my first experience with death. I didn't understand it. I genuinely didn't realize that I wouldn't ever see my great-grandmother again in this life. Because I had never had the experience before, my choices on how to interpret this event were limited. Other adults tried to explain to me what had occurred and what it really meant, but I still didn't have the personal experience to grasp the event.

That was my first experience with death.

My grandmother just died recently. She was the last of my grandparents. There has been quite a space of time between the passing of my great-grandmother and my grandmother. Within several decades, I have witnessed many people close and extremely close to me pass away. I have lost a nephew who was 18 months old, several of my aunts and uncles, my other grandparents, many close friends and other extended family members.

Since the first experience of death in my family, I have had multiple occasions to think of the transition from this life to the afterlife. I have had time to form beliefs and opinions regarding the event we call death. I have been able to make peace with it. Although I don't have all of the answers surrounding the passing of a loved one, I hold a perspective that gives me peace.

When the death of someone near to me occurs, I have the power to make more choices on how I will interpret those moments. As a child without experiences, I had few choices. Now I have many. **The difference is experience.**

I apologize that this might seem like a grim example, but it is one interpretation of how to look at death. On the other hand, it can be seen as a time to celebrate the contributions of an amazing human being.

The point I want to stress here is that as **we grow in our experiences**, we find more ways to choose how to interpret a situation.

Perhaps another example of this might help explain this concept further. I was raised in Calgary, Alberta in Canada. Growing up, we didn't really do a lot of exotic traveling. Most of the world I'd seen up until that point happened on road trips and camping with my family. I had a very narrow perspective of the world. I almost thought that my relatively small and down to earth city was the center of the universe. The choices that I considered with those limited experiences were also confined and small.

I remember when I began to travel around my 19th birthday; I had the opportunity to live in France and Belgium. This was my first real time outside of my own community for any length of time. My entire perspective on life changed. You might even say at the outset that I had a little culture shock.

Following that experience, I went to school for two years in the United States. Later, I had a chance to live in China for a year. Each experience with new lands, culture and people expanded my experience. Now as I think about perspective, beliefs and the ability to choose, I almost laugh at how naive I was as a young teenager, thinking that my world was the center of the universe. My knowledge and awareness were so limited back then.

I have now had the liberty to travel to nearly every major city on the globe, and my perspective has expanded even more. In fact, as I am writing this chapter, I am presently on an airplane traveling home from New York City. Talk about an environment very different from the Canadian city I was raised in! The interesting thing about perspective is I have grown to love so many more things because my perspective has grown and risen so much.

 POWER THOUGHT: The language we attach to our experiences dictates the kind of experiences we have.

Expanding Your Perspective is a Principle of Power

Obviously, the more you experience, the more effective you will be at discovering who you are and what you believe. This also gives more power in interpreting events and, as we will discuss later, acting on them. **The more you expand, the more you have to draw on for answers when you need them.**

We will talk later about how to use these experiences, resources and relationships to build more success in your life, but for now, I want to encourage you to seek out experiences. Look for opportunities that you can learn from and expand your experience. I specifically love the idea of expanding through travel, as it is a powerful way to look at how others in our world think, act and solve problems. Diversity is to be celebrated, and you can learn so much through excursions in towns, cities, states and countries. We live in an amazing world, and the more experiences you have, the more I am convinced you will see and believe that **amazing things are possible.**

Let's Talk About Belief

Belief is an idea or concept that you allow to paint your perspective. That's right. I said allow. Whether you recognize it or not, you choose the beliefs you will hold as your own. You also choose what you will *not* believe. Both of these aspects of belief (what you will or will not endorse) have a profound effect on what you will do.

Belief is almost like a dimmer switch, meaning that the things you believe are held at different levels of commitment or conviction. Not everything we believe has the same value. We will be talking about this in more detail when we get to the power of values, but right now, I want to say that we always act in harmony with the beliefs we value most and will often compromise beliefs that are valued less.

The value of beliefs can also change based on experiences we have or sometimes who we surround ourselves with. You've heard the idea of peer pressure. Kids deemed less popular will often follow the actions of the favored crowds just to be accepted, even if they wouldn't normally engage in these actions outside of the pressure. The belief or value of belonging to a group is more important to our personal convictions. We will also talk more about this powerful concept later.

One thing certain about belief is that it shapes our efforts and actions. When we believe that something is possible, or that the fruits of our efforts will produce the desired result, we are more likely to take action. **When our belief lacks strength, our efforts will also be weak.** When outcomes are expected of us by others, yet we do not have the same beliefs, we do not perform well. This can be seen in companies where a manager imposes goals on those they supervise. When activities are required from us that we do not value or believe in, we give less than our sincerest efforts.

Beliefs Create Standards

Standards are the beliefs about what we require as absolutes in our lives. We wake up and go about our days according to our standards. Beliefs dictate and create the standards we find acceptable. When something is below our standards, we will strive to have those needs met. **Yes, standards are a real need.**

However, when our standards have been reached, we are no longer motivated to reach higher.

For this reason, one of the things I ask students in our live PPM sessions to do is to investigate the standards that they believe they are worthy of. Most people fall short of living a stellar life because they settle for a lower standard. Once that lower standard has been met, they feel somewhat content. They become acclimated to "just good enough." Although they will express a desire to have more, their standards deny it.

Exercise: Take a moment and consider how the standards you have set for your life have determined the reality you experience. Are there areas of your life where you would like to raise your standard? Are there areas of your life where you truly believe you deserve more or are living at a level less than you are entitled to?

If that is the case, identify areas where you could make some immediate changes in what your standards are.

Expectations

An expectation is a form of belief. When we expect something to happen, we have a strong belief that the expectation will appear in reality. When we expect an outcome, we dedicate ourselves to it and will often make accommodations in our lives to receive what we expected. Later in the book, I will share how expectations are also the source of all human frustration, negative emotion, negative reaction, and often interpersonal conflict. **Expectation is powerful.**

When we expect an event or circumstance, we line up our beliefs and actions to support those expectations. It is one of the strongest forms of belief that we experience. When we truly believe in an outcome, we will often change our behaviors and actions to fulfill those outcomes.

The interesting thing about your beliefs is that you will also prepare for and accommodate negative expectations too. **We truly create what we expect will happen.**

A friend of mine was recently involved in a car accident. As I spoke to her about it later, she said that it was all a result of someone forgetting to turn off their signal light. Everyone involved in the collision had the expectation that the instigating driver was actually going to do what they had indicated with the signal light. Expectation, when it is firmly believed, always creates action. In this case, other drivers proceeded to follow their expectations, and it wound up in a multi-car collision.

I often work with companies and their sales teams. It is interesting to see that when a salesperson feels prepared, believes in his/her product and departs the office expecting success, success follows. Even when a salesperson has all of the essentials – product knowledge, company support, excellent sales scripts and glossy materials – if they falter in their feelings of preparation, belief and expectation, they fail.

People create the outcomes they believe in and expect.

Standards, Beliefs and Expectations Follow Influence

We will spend more time later in the book talking about the power of the things and people you surround yourself with. For now, it is important that I point out that your standards and beliefs are shaped and influenced by what and whom you choose to surround yourself with.

Traditionally, most personal development materials focus on how important it is that you surround yourself with excellent people and strong mentors and coaches if you want to reach higher levels in your life. Those things are important, but influence isn't just about people. As I said, we will speak in greater detail about this in another chapter, but I want to take a moment now to invite you to consider that everything you allow in your life is an influence (the television that you watch, the time you spend on the internet, the books you read, the places you frequent). Everything you choose to spend your time with has an influence on the standards and beliefs of what you expect out of life for yourself and what you believe possible for yourself.

 POWER THOUGHT: Surround yourself with amazing people and situations, and you will rise to an amazing life.

Exercise: Again, I am going to share more on this subject later in the book, so I struggled to determine whether I would include this exercise here or later in the book. As you can see, it made it here. My reasoning is that your influences shape your standards and beliefs to such a powerful degree that I felt it was important that we begin to look at what is shaping your life as quickly as possible.

I would like you to spend the next few days carefully observing your surroundings, how you spend your time and whom you spend it with. Evaluate these influences and even give them a rating between 1 and 10 depending on whether they are helping you to create positive standards in your life or pulling you down to compromise. Are they creating a greater belief in yourself and your possibilities, or are they keeping you stagnant and holding you back?

Changing your surroundings is one of the fastest ways to change your state and your expectations of what you can create in your life.

Questions on Perception and Belief to Consider:

1. How do our beliefs influence our perception of reality?

2. How do our standards shape our reality?

3. How do our beliefs and expectations create our standards?

4. How are standards, beliefs and expectations influenced by our surroundings?

5. What in your surroundings is influencing you in positive ways?

6. What in your surroundings is influencing you in negative ways?

7. What can you change in your influences right now that would improve your beliefs and expectations?

8. How does what we expect shape our outcomes?

CHAPTER FIVE

The Power of Change

Somewhere inside us all is the power to change the world.

- Roald Dahl

You have the power to grow

It is not possible to grow without change

Without change you become obsolete

Mark Twain was once quoted as saying the only person who likes change is a wet baby. I guess that describes most people as they face change. Many have the idea that change is hard work and requires us to be uncomfortable. As I observed the world's top achievers, I believe **choosing to change is actually easier work than staying the same.** Those who do the work of changing to improve themselves enjoy freedom, unlike the ones who dig in their heels and resist change.

The fact of the matter is that the world around us is constantly changing. **Change is the only thing that is constant.** We see this every day in our personal and professional lives. Disasters (natural and human-made), relationships, technology, businesses closing down – it is all around us. Since the days of Socrates, it has been said that there is no such thing as a plateau in life. You are either growing or you are in a state of decay. Both of these states will involve work. Obviously, with growth, work is found at the beginning with the efforts of learning new skills, a commitment of time, money and effort, and oftentimes a significant stretching to learn and create new habits. However, the result is eventually freedom.

As I stated before, the world around us is changing at a pace faster than we have ever experienced before. Our choices aren't about whether we will change but rather how fast we can change. *Those who embrace change and live on the edge of it create more success and achieve more. If you don't change, you become obsolete.*

Be Proactive

For those individuals who choose to remain the same, they may seem to have it easy upfront by doing very little work or nothing at all, but eventually, their inactivity leaves them in a state of catch up or pain while facing the consequences that now await them. Let me put it this way. There are those who resist change. That is a choice. There are those who claim that they are staying the same (business as usual, in a sense). That is also a choice. Whether you want to or not, change still takes place.

For those who choose to be ahead of the curve, they do their work as change unfolds. Often, they are considered innovators. They are rewarded as early adopters and considered proactive. On the other end of the spectrum, it appears that the ones who resist change don't have as much work to do, but the truth is that their efforts are much heavier, stressful and intense. I am reminded of the saying that states we can either "pay now and play later, or we can play now but will have to pay later." Many people choose to pay later and end up discovering that the late payment is accompanied by interest. **Catch up is always harder than proactive prevention.**

To provide a real-life example, I observed this spectrum in the financial life of two separate friends. The first one was always quick to adjust to what was happening to his business. He implemented new technologies and learned as much as he could about industry trends and customer behavior. It wasn't easy work, but he was a leader in his industry. On the other hand, my second friend resisted adopting modern implementations. He often labeled things (e.g., the internet and social media) as fads that wouldn't stick around that long. He waited, watched and claimed that he was being cautious to make sure something would stick around before using it.

My innovator friend worked hard in advance and was able to take advantage of opportunities that appeared. He became very wealthy as a result. My other friend was always playing catch up due to his choices. Consequently, he has been forced to pay premiums to get up to speed, push harder to catch up, and has lost many customers because he simply couldn't service their needs properly and adequately.

There is another saying, similar to the one earlier, which says, "Pay now and play later with interest. Or play now and pay later with interest." This is true in the case of my two friends.

One of the blessings with the concept of change is to realize that no matter what your current situation is right now, you have the choice to deny it entry into your life. You can change your present situation, and you have the power within you to do so. You can't change what you won't own. **For change to be effective, you must own and take responsibility for your situation.** You can't successfully change anything if you seek to blame what you wish to revise in your daily life on others. This goes for behaviors as well as professional activities. When a person takes individual ownership, everything can change for the better, including relationships, finances, company culture, sales and even self-esteem. All things can be improved once the decision is made to take ownership and personal responsibility.

Let me say here that while you cannot alter all of the outcomes you've experienced in the past and may even be enduring some of the consequences of those situations, you can certainly start creating new outcomes immediately.

Because change is such a crucial topic and the most common reason people come to me for help and life strategizing, I want to share a few things I've observed about change that you might not have spent a lot of time considering.

 POWER THOUGHT: You can't go back and change the beginning, but you could start from here and change the ending. - C.S. Lewis

Embrace Change to Achieve Success

Naturally, not all changes support what you want to do and where you want to go. Some changes can take you away from your goal instead of toward it. Some changes can hurt and cause sadness in your life. Some changes involve loss. Oftentimes those changes are not ones that you create intentionally, and many times they occur as a result of circumstances beyond your immediate control. However, there is a change that you will deliberately create and seek out. It's a way of telling the universe, "see I can do this too", when things go wrong.

Then you can go and deliberately create change with purpose to reach the outcomes that you wish to achieve.

Change is a prerequisite to success. If you are not determined to seek out and embrace change, you will never have the power to receive success. If you think about it, this makes perfect sense when you recognize that the choices of your past have created your reality. Simply put, if you want a new situation, you need to do something different. There is a popular phrase which states that **if you always do what you've always done, you'll always get what you've always gotten.** It appears true, but it's actually worse than that. If you always do what you've always done, and do it in a world that is changing and evolving around you, your results are going be outdated and obsolete; therefore, you won't likely receive what you had gotten before with those same results.

If you think about technology again, for example, you can see what I am referring to. It is not enough to know "basic computer skills" in the job market; you are expected to be proficient in a multitude of programs, and they just keep coming (look at how cellphones have evolved over the decades). If you make a conscious choice to keep at the same level you have always been at, many facets of your life will become antiquated, just like some of those old computer programs.

Change requires internal and external commitments. In other words, *change will require a new way of thinking, a new way of looking at things, and a new way of processing ideas and information as you encounter it.* However, it does not stop there. You need to take action to be involved in creating change through making decisions, taking action and adjusting your course when it is required.

Change is Your Power

The good news here is that you hold the power of change within you. If you don't like an aspect of your life, you have the power to change it. You can make new decisions, develop new habits, keep new company, and make choices in any other aspect of your life.

You have **limitless options** as to what changes you would like to make in your life. The only limits are really your imagination. In this regard, change is one of the gateways to all of the possibilities in your future.

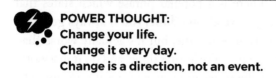

POWER THOUGHT:
Change your life.
Change it every day.
Change is a direction, not an event.

The ability to change is almost like going to the biggest department store there ever was (or think of the Mall of America, the biggest in the country). Yet instead of having just choices of clothing, shoes, cosmetics, toys, housewares and whatever else you normally find, you can also find every possible choice you could ever consider. You can have anything you want. All you have to do is take the changes that go with it.

What an epic realization!

Choose what you want. Take it to the checkout and make the changes that each outcome requires and the outcome is yours. It's that simple! At least it should be. Most people end up leaving many of the things they really want because they don't know how to choose the changes that they should in order to pay for the outcome.

Sometimes people don't like the word change. I'm not sure why it freaks some people out, but it does. If you're one of those people, that's okay. Try thinking in terms of these other words: **adapt, acclimate, accommodate, come around, return to source, revise, readjust, modify, alter, harmonize, recalibrate.** These words are all really good descriptions of what you are trying to accomplish through change.

Progressive Change Requires Harmony

Progressive change doesn't just occur because you think you deserve good things to happen to you. I mentioned in an earlier chapter that I had the opportunity to speak in a maximum security prison in North Carolina. I've spoken in a few prisons to the inmates, and one observation that seems to be pretty consistent is that most of the people in there felt they were making the best decisions to create good outcomes at the time they were making them. In other words, they had the very best intentions.

Intentions are not enough. Intentions (as demonstrated by the folks in prison) can even hurt people – even good intentions. For change and choice to produce progressive and empowering change, they must be based on correct principles. **These correct principles are laws.**

The universe follows a very predictable set of laws. To illustrate what I mean, let's use the law of gravity as an example. Everyone experiences it and is subject to that law. Regardless of your intentions or desires, you cannot bend the law of gravity to excuse yourself from its effects. If you jump up, you will come back down. It's just the law and your feelings about it are irrelevant.

Obviously, when you understand the law of gravity, you can use that law to sit down or fly in an airplane. It is interesting that some people say there is no gravity in space. Those who understand physics know that the mathematics and principles behind gravity actually do still exist in space; they simply manifest themselves in different ways because of new variables.

There are specific laws that will result in happiness. But when they are violated, they create the opposite effect.

There are specific laws that result in self-confidence, self-worth, personal fulfillment, wealth and abundance, better relationships, a healthy lifestyle and whatever else you may desire. When those laws are violated they create the opposite.

While the specific laws of creating the outcomes you want can and do vary, here are some universal laws that apply to all positive outcomes you may wish to create.

Outcomes are the Result of Ownership

As I interviewed the world's top achievers, I found almost every one of them was a person who owned his or her roots. Even before any possible outcome was on the horizon, they understood that if they gave away the power to own their situation and make the changes they desired, they would lose their desired outcome.

Instead, **they owned who they were, the mistakes that they had made, and they did not blame others**. If there was a situation where someone else was involved, they did not point the finger at the other individual involved. Rather, they first looked at how their efforts and activities created or contributed to the challenge. Then they looked at how they could change things.

This is very different from most people, who point the blame immediately at others and, in doing so, give all the power for change or correction away. **If you *own* it, you can *change* it**. If you blame it, you can't claim it. Period. We can take ownership of what's going on in our lives and make new choices. We can raise our standards of what we will accept and how we will act in return.

How do you initiate change and know specifically what you should change?

Let's start first with what you should change. How do you recognize what activities are working against your results? How do you know what you are doing that could be improved immediately? The simple answer to this question is actually found much earlier in the book. We know what isn't on track, but need to truly understand what track we want to be on.

Once we know the specific outcomes and feelings we're trying to create, we can recognize where we are off target. Your knowledge of what you change will grow as you begin to live in greater harmony with the things you really want to create. As you become committed and start moving toward the things you want, the things you don't want will begin to become more apparent.

Changing these things will come down to a careful choice and an emotionally charged commitment to do things differently. As we have discussed earlier, when we have a powerful reason for why and one that especially connects with our emotions, we have a stronger ability to stay consistent with that change.

Change also occurs as we recognize that we have alternative choices to what we have done in the past. You'll remember that choice was the first and foundational principle of PPM. When we start to recognize we have choices in real life, we begin to see that change is much more possible for us. We also begin to recognize that as we get more comfortable with change on a consistent basis, we begin to explore our options for change more frequently in the real world.

POWER THOUGHT: Lasting change always begins with a vision of a better, positive and compelling future.

Change is the Result of Influence

Change is most often the result of influence. What we allow to influence us shares the idea of what is possible. Possibilities enable us to recognize alternatives to what we are currently thinking and ultimately act on. *If you want to improve your ability to make and cope with changes, then level up the things that you are allowing to influence you.*

Take out the goals that you created earlier in this book. If those things are what you truly want, you'll find that change need not be frightening. In fact, change can be something that you love because you will be moving closer to who and what you want to become.

Change is a tool. **Change, when used properly, should be defined as an improvement.** When you are changing to move closer to the things that you really want in life, it is a blessing and not a curse. **Creating a successful life is simply a matter of revision and shifting ideas and behavior.**

One definition I saw about change was interesting. *It is an ongoing process of evolving into what you'll leave behind.* Because, by the time you get there, you'll be done with that particular "growth spurt" and leave that behind too. It reminds me of how a caterpillar metamorphoses into the butterfly. The cocoon, which is left behind, is a symbol of the change that has taken place.

A powerful examination that I have observed many times in the real world is how often people hold themselves back from fully experiencing the benefits of change by determining to carry the cocoon with them. They are no longer as they were; yet, they can't let go of past hurt, challenges, mistakes or guilt. The imagery of carrying the cocoon is pretty accurate considering most of those who carry their past find value in either sharing with everyone they meet or carrying their cocoon so high and proud that people can't help but notice.

Another problem that many people experience when it comes to change is that they try to change the consequences rather than the cause. The outcomes change as a result of changing how they were created. That means sometimes you have to ask the important questions regarding what created those outcomes. What were the roots?

Most people are afraid or unwilling to face the roots. In our live events of PPM we have a saying that we share, "If you own it, you can change it." The first step to escaping feelings of self-doubt, a lack of worthiness or concern is the same step that is required to create progress. You must own your roots. **Once you own the cause of the effect, you can change the effect.**

 POWER THOUGHT: Most people try to change the consequences of their reality instead of the cause of it.

Here is a side note about influences. If you have changed your outcomes through what has influenced you, you can also lose your outcomes by influence. What you choose to surround yourself with can also rob you of progress that you have made.

When I was in high school, I saw this first-hand with a guy I had grown up with. He had been in my kindergarten class all the way through elementary school and then through middle school. We ultimately wound up in the same class in high school. I was always slightly jealous of this guy's ability to get good grades so easily. He was a math genius, a science genius, an athletic genius and quite frankly a genius everywhere else (including with the girls). Like I said, I was jealous.

You most likely already know where this story is going. He fell in with the wrong crowd and they began to influence him. He started using drugs and his grades and abilities immediately began to suffer. Everything in his life became subject to his new influences.

Here's the end of this tragic story: One of the most promising leaders in my school ended up being asked to leave without completing his education. He continued allowing these influences to lead him away from his greatest self. I recently heard that he was going back to jail for robbing a gas station. I am not jealous anymore; instead, I'm really sad.

Change Always Produces Results

I touched on this notion above, but I really think it's worth mentioning again. You want progressive change, and change actually has the ability to produce three different kinds of results: pain, pleasure and possibilities. Which will you choose or give permission to come into your life? One of these outcomes happens mostly by not making a choice; the other two require it.

Change is rarely easy and is always uncomfortable. It is something new that you have never encountered before. It is only natural that it might cause you to feel a bit awkward. I like to think of it akin to jumping into a swimming pool. At first, it feels very cold and can startle the system the instant you get in. However, if you stay committed to not climbing out right away, even for just a little while, you adjust and can have a really fun time. Change will always be strange, but decide to do it anyway.

 POWER THOUGHT: You must be willing to let go of where you are to where you are going. Don't let past frustrations keep you from future victories.

Change Has a Learning Curve

Any time we are attempting something new, or we are introduced to something different than what we are used to, there is a learning curve. All deliberate growth occurs in the form of a J curve. A J curve is an educational term that describes how things are learned. Essentially the J curve is a pattern that says how we learn things appears in the shape of a J. We start at the tiny hook at the bottom, and at the beginning, we struggle.

As we continue to learn, we descend around the bend at the bottom, and if we persist and push and keep going, we eventually round the learning curve at the bottom of the J. Then we begin to ascend the back stem of the J, upward toward competency. You'll also notice how the back stem of the J rises vertically and straight up quite quickly and steadily as you exit the bottom hook. This is where you really begin to experience success, flow and growth. Simple, yet profound.

Unfortunately, most people stop just at the point of the first bend. A little bit of difficulty stops them, and they become convinced that the resistance experienced is a sign that they can't do what they set out to accomplish. Instead, it is a sign that you are just about to do your set thing better. The reason why most people stop making the changes required of them is that they lose sight of their purpose.

 POWER THOUGHT: Progressive change requires a constant connection to purpose.

There's an old saying that **every master was once a disaster**. This first curve is the disaster before the master.

When we expect that there will be some resistance and difficulty, we can greet it when it arrives and know that we are right on track.

As an interesting side note, as I researched the experiences of the top achievers and observed the experiences of thousands of my students over the years, I have noticed that the time spent at the bottom part of the J curve is a lot shorter than most people expect or realize. With dedicated effort, most individuals can push through the learning struggles and experience degrees of competence in a very short time. *The difference between those who struggle for a long time and those who move through the learning curve can be accelerated through a positive attitude, focusing on the outcomes, and a **willingness to adapt** their approaches.*

You've heard that nothing worth having happens or stays easily. I am not sure I totally agree with this idea. While I believe in hard work and consistent effort, my experience has been that if you start right and push through to get momentum doing it right, it is much less complicated than most people believe.

Regular Change is Necessary for Growth

One kind of change frustrates me regularly, but I accept that it is for my own good. I'm not great with technology. At least that's what it feels like sometimes. Every time I seem to have something figured out, I suddenly get a notice that I need to update my device (I addressed evolving technology in business earlier). Whether it's my phone, laptop, iPad or an app that I'm using, it seems like I'm getting constant updates. I usually think to myself about why I need an update; it's working just fine the way that it is. A few times as I've uttered this phrase, I have had to stop and remind myself that this is exactly the way many of my students feel.

Often they think that things are going perfectly the way they are and there is no reason for an update. I have felt that way a few times with my technology.

Recently I had an interesting experience with one of my devices. The warning to update came quite a while back. I decided to ignore it. I liked how things were going and I felt that I would be fine without it. Month after month, the warning appeared and I just dismissed it. I liked the way things were and changing things frightened me.

Soon I started getting documents, attachments and invitations from others that I could not open. I found that not being able to open some of these materials robbed me of timely invitations, opportunities, the information I needed and even collecting money transfers. Ultimately, **my desire to resist updating my operating systems kept me back and left me behind.**

This is very much like our life. We may choose to remain stagnant as everyone and everything around us changes, but soon (especially at the fast pace our world is moving today), we will be left behind.

A friend of mine observed the other day that it is not enough to use as an excuse that you are a senior citizen. Even seniors are becoming highly proficient in their use of technology. Very similar to life, as long as you are breathing, you must seek out and embrace progressive change.

If your changes are not working as you wish, or you feel stuck, I have found that there are generally six things that you might want to look at and possibly alter.

Motive: This is the most common reason why most attempts to change don't work. If you are looking to create lasting change in your life, they must be attached to your highest values. *As you determine how change is tied to your highest desires, you will have power to stay committed to the changes you are trying to make.* Often people fail to make and sustain changes because they are based on how they think they should be to please others, or they are asked to change by others. As I shared above, you need to own it in order to change it. You will never own a change unless you see purpose or value in doing so.

Strategy: Often a person may have great intentions and strong desires to make a change that resonates with his/her highest value, but there is still failure. Often this is a result of following incorrect strategies. As discussed above, success is based on following a specific set of laws that correspond to the outcome you want to create.

Speed: Speed of implementations can sometimes be the reason changes do not work. Believe it or not, most often the problem with speed isn't going too slow; rather, it's going too fast. I have seen many of the students who have attended my seminars crash and burn, so to speak, because they have been too quick and aggressive to make changes. Consequently, they ended up not building a sustainable foundation.

Too much: Focusing on too much and biting off more than you can chew can also prevent you creating the changes that you want to make. Try to take on change one day at a time and focus on making changes in manageable moments, not colossal shifts. **Big power most often appears in small changes.**

Traveling companions: While I am not directly referring to people that are influencing you, they are generally the ones who make the biggest difference. If you want to level up your life, you must level up the people you share it with. Later in the book, we will talk in more detail about networks, relationships and influence. But for now, all I'm going to say is if change isn't happening as quickly as you'd like, take a look at who is tagging along with you.

Direction: Sometimes the biggest challenge with the changes you are trying to create is that they are taking you in the wrong direction. We talked earlier about the outcomes you want in your life. What we didn't stress is the importance of authenticity. **If you are pursuing something that isn't authentic to you, it will be difficult.** Creating changes that are fundamentally different from what you sincerely and authentically desire will cause you to experience resistance and hardship. Take a careful look at what you really want and the most important answer to those questions will always come from within you rather than an external source. **Going in the wrong direction always leads to challenges in creating or maintaining changes.**

Even though this chapter is about the importance of change, and that when things are going well you should embrace change, I wanted to throw a wrench in all of that by saying that sometimes there are items that you should hang on to. Not everything needs to be changed. **Your best self and the things that you're doing that are working really well should never get lost in an attempt to change things that aren't working well.** I'm not going to say much more about that except to say that it will take some self-exploration and wisdom to determine what that is.

The biggest obstacle to real change is fear and frustration. Once you shift your focus from your purpose to fear or frustration, progressive change is difficult to create. Don't let yourself become paralyzed into inactivity.

Questions About Change to Consider:

1. What changes do you need to make to get to your specific outcomes?

2. What is keeping you from making those changes?

3. What influences can help you make the changes permanent?

4. What laws do you need to learn to create outcomes you are seeking?

5. Are you motivated to create and maintain the changes you're seeking to create?

6. Are you using correct strategies to create the outcomes you want?

7. Are you rushing to create change when building it slower will work better?

8. Are your influences (especially the people you spend time with) helping you to create the changes you are seeking?

9. Are the changes you are trying to create authentic to who you are or really want?

10. What fears are keeping you from change?

11. How will you break through frustrations as you encounter them?

CHAPTER SIX

The Power of Values

It's not hard to make decisions once you know what your values are.

- Roy E. Disney

You will not make progress unless you stick to your path

Short-term values rarely produce long-term results

You create what you will accept

Tim came to my event with a problem. It's a common dilemma that many entrepreneurs experience. As our "mike runner" passed him the microphone at one of our seminars, Tim began to explain, "I am tired of chasing my tail to make ends meet. I've tried everything in business. I've tried *every* business I can think of. I've been in nearly every network marketing company, I've worked commission sales for major companies, I've been a consultant, a coach, a speaker, and I've started at least seven or eight businesses in the last four years. It seems that no matter what I try, I can't make any of them work. My wife has had enough, and she's on the verge of leaving. And I don't know what to do."

When he paused, I could see the frustration on his face. As I thought about all of the answers that I could give to him, the one that came most to my mind even caught me off guard.

Tim's problem was **authenticity of purpose**. Over the years, I have seen many people shift dramatically between ideas, strategies, jobs and even relationships. The problem generally occurs because they are seeking something they value in sources that won't provide it. Ultimately, they can't make progress because they aren't motivated to stick with something long enough to get traction. So they often hop from one good opportunity to another before creating anything of substance. They leave before the reward arrives.

People who follow this pattern believe they value money and often make poor choices of how to get it. I'm not necessarily saying these people are pursuing a path of dishonesty, although that does occur sometimes. What I am saying is that they gravitate to what they believe will provide that need in the quickest, easiest way, sometimes the laziest way, possible.

This is most likely where that saying, "Beware of get rich quick schemes" came from.

As I talked through the idea of authenticity of purpose and finding true values with Tim, he began to see that while the money was a big part of the lure, his truest values ironically centered upon having the freedom in his life to spend time with his family. Not just on weekends but any time he chose.

He additionally recognized that he highly valued diversity in everything he did, which meant that any vocation or business that kept him doing the same thing repeatedly would never work. He was an "ideas" man and felt alive only when working on something new. Through some of the exercises that followed at the seminar, he further recognized that he did not have to execute every idea that he created. With the support of others during some group work that day, he discovered that he was a master at coming up with creative ways to share his ideas so that others got excited. One of the ways he did this was through branding and marketing. Every single idea and company that he had created or been involved with up until that point had one thing in common: the marketing and graphics looked amazing.

As Tim considered his values, he recognized that following this particular path would give him the time he desired with his family, the ability to tap into the ideas person that he was and connect it directly to a talent he had.

Fast forward six years later, and currently he is the successful and prosperous owner of a digital and print marketing agency that has several people working for him.

When we find our authentic purpose, which is in line with our highest values, everything becomes easier.

POWER THOUGHT: If we don't take the time to discover our important long-term values we will become distracted by our short-term wants.

Circumstances Often Determine Our Immediate Values

Immediate values are a set of short-term values that dictate our immediate behavior. In some circumstances, this can provide temporary relief, but it rarely produces long-term satisfaction.

In some ways, it reminds me of Maslow's hierarchy of needs. At the bottom, you find basic survival needs, and at the top is self-realization. You don't really think too much about self-realization when you're about to be eaten by a lion. **The essentials must be satisfied before we can start mediating with power.**

Remember at the beginning of this book we talked about the **five pillars of success: self, spirituality, health, relationships and abundance.** It has been interesting over the last few decades to watch these pillars manifest themselves at my seminars. Not everyone expresses the five as equally important in their life. In fact, by asking what a person's most important goals are, I have found that they have changed based on what is currently going on in that individual's life.

When someone is struggling with finances, for example, abundance becomes the most important goal. If they are struggling with aspects of their relationships, that becomes the priority. If it's an issue with their health, then wellbeing becomes the main pursuit. *The lesson is that most people place a high value on what they feel they lack.* In other words, I have found without exception that if you are feeling unbalanced or lacking in one of these pillars, it shifts to become one of your primary goals.

I presume that's one area where I think Maslow's work could be expanded on. He says survival is the first essential need that we satisfy. I say, it depends.

We have many examples of people who have given their lives to protect a loved one. That means that the pillar of relationship in that circumstance was more important than self.

We have examples of people that have gone on hunger strikes to be sure their philosophy was recognized. That means a person's health was placed second to the mission of self.

We have more than enough examples of people who put money and abundance above relationships, health, self-fulfillment and spirituality.

While there are temporary circumstances and situations that will cause us to alter our authenticity of purpose and highest values, we will only find lasting happiness as we return to them quickly and consistently.

Incorrect Values and Inauthentic Purposes

It is very possible, as we saw with Tim in the above situation, to find yourself pursuing incorrect values and an inauthentic path. Obviously, no one forced him on to this path, but he did find himself there because of the influences around him. Our society structures ideas around us that we accept as truth, which is not necessarily in harmony with who we really are and what we find value in.

Recently, I conducted training on abundance and wealth, in London. As the attendees arrived and we began a discussion about affluence, I heard comments that were clearly competitive. The ideas around riches were very much directed to material things, net worth and cash on hand. Now don't get me wrong. I am not against accumulating these things, but as people dove deeper into their more authentic selves and felt safe to do so, the definition of wealth and abundance began to change for the majority present in the room.

Most in the group actually began to recognize that they were already wealthy. The difference was that their wealth had been manifesting in the ways that they truly valued more than the money or material things they placed so much significance on.

Now here's the interesting part: when you really know what you value, and you have authenticity of purpose, you can actually have both.

Our Values Are Our Standards

Our standards dictate the lifestyle and situations we create in our lives. If we truly believe something is intolerable, we fix it. If we can live with it according to the standards we have set for ourselves, then we live with it. Our values determine our standards. **We always raise the level of our expectations and standards to the level of our values.**

If you want to live a better life, raise your standards!

Exercise: What things do you experience in your life currently that you are not super excited about? Make a list of these things. I find it useful to use the five pillars as a guide. In your life, what things are you not really happy about with regard to the area of self? What about spirituality? Health? Relationships? Lastly, abundance?

Consider what standards you have for your activities around the things that created your current situations. There is a Chinese proverb that says, "If you would know your past, look at your current circumstances." This is very true when it comes to standards. We create what we will accept.

POWER THOUGHT:
You always create what you want most.

If you're not happy with your current circumstances, then it is time to make some new decisions about what you will accept in your life and what you will not. In other words, **it is time to raise your standards**. I encourage those in our live seminars to write an agreement as to what they will and will not accept in their lives going forward.

I am always surprised to see some of the situations people have been willing to accept. Probably one of the most powerful changes in acceptable standards that I saw came from a lady named Linda. When she talked about her standard change with the group, she shared how up until that point she had been the victim of bullying in the workplace and mental abuse at home. At first, everyone worried about what "fighting back" might bring to her life. Would she create conflict and possibly escalate the challenge in these relationships? Would it be possible that some of it might even turn physical?

As I asked her about the consequences of her choices to raise her standard, she explained she wasn't worried too much about that. The people she had let abuse her actually weren't that mean, they had actually encouraged her to stick up for herself many times. The challenge she expressed is that she had low standards and low self-worth, and felt it wasn't in her power to make choices to raise those standards.

An interesting lesson about standards is this: *We teach people how to treat us.*

Believe it or not, we also teach the universe how to treat us by what we decide is acceptable and unacceptable.

POWER THOUGHT: Raise the bar for what you will accept, and you will level up what you can become.

Settling is One of the Greatest Enemies of Success

Like Linda, too many people settle and accept the situation they find themselves in. They worry that standing up for something (especially themselves) will just rock the boat. Our standards don't only dictate how others will treat us, they also affect our own behavior.

We set up our boundaries around our behavior by our own standards. They dictate our boundaries and what we will and won't do.

One of the disappointing things about this revelation is that **we often expect more from others than we do from ourselves.**

As I learned from the top achievers, I found that their perspective on this issue of settling was reversed from most people. They actually expected more from themselves than they did from others. That is a very empowered perspective, and if you think back to our chapter on thought, this is the empowered proactive approach. Start with expecting the best and then you will not be governed by or place blame on the things that are outside of you and most often outside of your control.

Our Highest Values Determine our Priorities

Although we may have many things that we value and consider important to us, we do have a hierarchy of what we value. Among things we find significant, we have an order and sequence to what we value most and make choices that support that.

Given a choice between two important things, we will always pick the one we find of most worth. This is a challenge that most people find themselves in. I believe that when many individuals are given a choice to make between activities, the easy choices are the obvious ones (television shows, recreational, etc.). They become more difficult when you have two situations opposing each other that are most valuable. In many cases, (in fact, most of them) the reason why lasting success is so challenging for many people to achieve is that these kinds of choices are very tough. *Most people can't sacrifice what they value at the moment for what they might value more in the long term.*

Our Values Influence Our Urgency

We always prioritize what we value the most. At times, this can serve you well; at other times, this can create challenges. I have worked with people trying to create greater success in their lives, and it is not uncommon to see those who know what they need to do but refrain from doing certain tasks by choosing easy activities on their must-do list. In other words, their values are not totally committed to their final outcome because they place more value on being comfortable and following the easy path. Think of the entrepreneurial path. It takes a lot of self-discipline and hard work to continue building a business or multiple businesses, but often some will choose a less arduous career simply because it's less effort and complication.

Our Values Influence How We Do Things

In addition to affecting priorities, our values will also dictate how we approach problem solving and tactics we will entertain. Our values dictate the rules we play by in trying to create the outcomes we are hoping to achieve.

As I conducted my interviews with the top movers and shakers (along with observations of many who lacked success), it became clear that even those with the same objectives for their outcomes chose different rules. When values become more about the outcome than our ethics, oftentimes people will compromise their ethics. When you are solely focused on your results, you can make costly and, in extremes, even criminal mistakes to attempt to get to your desired outcomes. Placing a higher value on your outcomes than your ethics will cause you to seek shortcuts and shortsighted compromises.

Sometimes things do take time, and alternatives that violate the natural laws that we talked about in the last chapter often bring regret. The outcome may have been noble, but the method defeated the purpose, and even with the outcome, no success was created.

I believe it's also important to notice that our values dictate how we do things, meaning the quality of our efforts. When we truly value the activity we are engaged in, we perform it better and raise the standard of the work itself.

Picture a master craftsman. The highest value creates the highest passion, which in turn creates a commitment to excellence. Excellency is a reoccurring attribute in all people who achieve greatness.

 POWER THOUGHT: Your highest values are the best standard to which you should measure your thoughts, activities, and actions.

Values Dictate Boundaries and Influence your Decisions

As I said earlier, we make decisions and set our boundaries in ways that we believe serve us best and guard our values. Learning how to establish boundaries is what allows us to stay focused on what matters most to us. When we have no personal borders, we find that we can easily become distracted by every new opportunity or situation in front of us.

Most often, this can appear in the form of someone needing help. We've all experienced how someone else's emergency becomes our fire. When our values are clear and our boundaries established, we don't allow ourselves to become consumed by everyone's personal flames.

One of my core values is helping people. I have even been accused at times of being a people pleaser. Maybe you're like me. I used to rush to the rescue whenever anyone needed my help. I became a habitual lifesaver. I soon found that it was nearly impossible to help everyone and still get anything done for myself. There just wasn't enough time, attention, money, etc. to go around.

As I thought about my value of helping people, I realized that the most powerful way I could help them was to teach them more self-reliance. They didn't need rescuing as much as I thought. Often, folks could be their own lifeguard.

In the process of investigating my own values and building boundaries, I found a stronger way to support them and still fulfill my highest values.

We should never let what we value most be replaced by the values of others. There is a way for both to be met in most cases.

Having said that, this meant that some who had been schooled to respond a certain way in the above situation needed retraining. I was the first one who needed new instruction. I devised memorized statements that I could trigger myself to say any time someone appealed to me for help. These were non-offensive things that let them know I cared but expressed the limited amount of support I would be able to give upfront. Yes, it was difficult at times to stick with these commitments, but we'll talk more in a later chapter about how to anchor those unfamiliar proclamations and actions. For now, just know that you need to have them, and in the end everyone involved will feel better about it.

There's the old saying that a lifeguard can't save others until they know how to swim. This is one of those times.

Creating Habits

You've probably read or seen in self-help books or materials somewhere that it takes 20 days to form a habit. I'm sure you have even heard that habits are hard to break, and it's a struggle to change lifelong habits. The last chapter about changes gave you some ideas of why change is necessary to create success, along with sharing some of the common reasons people struggle with new ideas. However, here's something I didn't mention that will change everything.

When we value something at a high level, it becomes a high priority. When we value something, we do it. When we value something, we make changes. If you wonder why you haven't been able to build a new habit or get rid of an old one, it all comes down to what you value most.

Sometimes you may be nurturing habits that you feel are going to serve what you value most. Sometimes those habits are counterproductive. On occasion, the habits you feel are good are keeping you from great.

Exercise: Consider your daily habits. Make a list of the things that you do each day. Which of these are contributing to the outcomes you wish to create and which are working against it? As you list your habits, consider how you are getting value from them and how you think they are contributing to the things you value most.

Self-leadership and Courage are a Result of Your Values

I once read an interesting anecdote about courage and values. It left such an impression on me that I share it quite often at our PPM seminars. I'd like to share it here. It goes like this:

There was a senior monk who sat with three of his disciples. He asked them a question, "What is courage?" The first disciple answered, "Courage is when you fight for those you care about." The senior monk then asked the second disciple. Eager to impress, he answered, "Courage is to stand for those who cannot defend themselves." The senior monk then asked the third disciple who also was hoping to share a profound answer. He stated, "Courage is to stand for an idea." The senior monk surprised them by revealing the answer, "Courage is love." The three disciples clearly did not understand, so he began. "You do not have the courage to fight for those you care about unless you experience love. You do not have the courage to defend the defenseless unless you love their cause. You cannot have the courage to defend a philosophy unless you love it."

We only have the courage to defend things that we value highly. Courage requires sacrifice, and we will never sacrifice things we don't care about for the things we care about most. Think of a family member who would rush back in a burning building to save a loved one, or a single parent working multiple jobs to save money for his/her children's education. **When we have something or someone we care about or value most, we are willing to sacrifice everything.**

Value it so much that you are willing to do what is hard. One of my success interviews was Edward James Olmos. You might know him as Commander Adama in the recent television adaptation of *Battlestar Galactica.* He has appeared in countless television shows and movies over the years. As I asked him about his definition of success, he said the following, "Some people like that success is doing what's hard. That's not how you create success. Success is finding something you love and then doing it even when it is hard."

When you find what you love, there will still be difficult days and moments that are hard. *You must have the courage to move forward even when it is not easy.*

 POWER THOUGHT: Love what you do, and obstacles will never deter you.

Exercise: How will you remind yourself to stay committed even when things are hard? Consider some strategies that you can create to remind yourself how much you love, value and are committed to creating the outcomes that you are striving for. How will you stay in integrity and maintain your values instead of chasing a shortsighted shortcut?

Recognizing Your Values

Recognizing your values and establishing standards is not always easy. Most people are unaware of their values, and when asked to share them, they deflect to what they think the correct answers are supposed to be. When I have asked this question in a seminar or group setting, the values in the room end up changing due to the influence of people they think have better answers. It becomes a competition to share who has the coolest responses.

Authenticity requires reflection and contemplation. I don't think it's because people don't want to put in the effort; rather, I believe the real challenge is that most people don't know where to start or what questions to ask. Even if they can identify a few of their significant values, they have no idea on how to identify which value means the most to them.

The Power of Your Why

A powerful way to discover your authenticity of purpose is to spend time contemplating your reasons why you want certain things in your life. You'll remember at the beginning of this book, I asked you to write down your most important goals and use a timer. These goals are important to you.

To find your values in your ambitions and make sure they are authentic, you need to ask yourself **why** you chose them. There are no wrong answers, but you must discover how they serve you. *The stronger the reason why gives you more power to reach your goals.*

Exercise: Take a look at some of the big decisions you have made recently. Consider what values were involved in you making that decision. How did that decision serve those values in your opinion? Why did that value lead to that decision? How did you feel that decision would serve that value? In other words, trace your decision all the way to your real reason why.

 POWER QUOTE: Your *will*power will come from your *why* power. If you can determine why something is important, it is more likely you *will* do it.

Once you have discovered your values, which are a reflection of your most significant reasons for why, you will have more willpower and commitment to creating more effective decisions.

Questions on Value to Consider:

1. What does authenticity of purpose mean to you?

2. What are your most important values?

3. What are the short-term values that you are seeking?

4. Is this related to what you feel like you are lacking?

5. Are you aware of your values?

6. How are your values creating your standards?

7. Where are you choosing to settle in your life?

8. How are you giving the power of your values to others?

9. How are you losing your own authenticity by living the values of the world?

10. How are you allowing your values to influence your decisions?

11. How do your values influence your habits?

12. Do you have the courage to stand for what you value most?

13. Why do some people fall out of integrity when it comes to creating their outcomes?

14. How can you be sure to do things correctly?

15. How are you a leader to yourself?

16. How does what you value most appear in your daily life?

17. How does what you value in the short term keep you from what you value in the long term?

18. How important are your reasons why?

CHAPTER SEVEN

The Power of the Present

*Ordinary people think merely
of spending time.
Great people think of using it.*

- Unknown

Learn to use the moment you have right now

If you want to control your life, control your time

Happiness exists in the present

The title of this chapter is a bit deceptive. At first, you may think that it has to do with a specific period of time known as the present. In one sense, this is true. The other aspect is really about how to use this moment.

The challenge that most people experience is that they neither recognize the fragility of that single moment in time nor utilize it in any beneficial way. Eventually, because of this neglect, they receive nothing in return. At the risk of sounding a bit juvenile, I should point out that the true present appears in how you use the present. Until you learn how to use **this moment,** you will never be able to change your situation.

Plans for the future, regret and longing for the past never makes anything happen. One of the success interviews I conducted revealed something interesting to me. The conversation was with a well-known writer. He had written novels, movies, and even television programs. I asked him about the hardest aspect of writing these high-profile projects and scripts. I began to think of the challenges of creating characters, finding unique and undiscovered settings, developing conflicts, and writing dialog true to the characters. I thought about creating moments that were memorable and interesting and all of the other stuff you'd think goes along with making an amazing story. However, he provided me with a surprising response.

He stated, "The hardest thing about writing is actually sitting down to write."

Since then, I have discovered that this statement holds true for many people. Most individuals know what they want, but they often have so many distractions of other things that they let occupy their present that they just simply never get around to going after what they truly want and desire.

Oftentimes, procrastination is blamed. I define **procrastination as a** *deliberate choice* **to put off something that you want to do** because another item has appeared that becomes the preferred option. Procrastination is a choice that people make because the task at hand is just not high enough in their values to complete.

Procrastination is not the only thief of dreams. I believe that many people simply don't recognize the time that is actually in their hands. These unique moments of now slip by unnoticed because they have made a choice to be unaware. **Remember, that which is not monitored appears less valuable.**

I have been surprised at how much time throughout a day, a week, a month and even a lifetime is lost in waiting, watching or surfing. *If you don't take control of your time, you will never have total control over your life.*

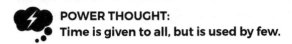

POWER THOUGHT:
Time is given to all, but is used by few.

At the risk of repeating something you've probably heard a million times, I still need to say it because it is important. **Every person alive today has the same 24 hours in their day!** I can't emphasize this point enough! All of us are given this same amount equally, and no matter how much money you have, how much influence you have in the world, no matter how many successes or failures come from your past, *you cannot earn more time.* In fact, even if you wanted to, you can't loan or borrow time. What you have, it's yours. (There is a way to leverage it, and we will talk about that later.) But you technically cannot expand the actual allotment of time you have.

The difference between the most successful and less successful people is found in how they utilize their time and how they get results in the shortest amount of time possible. I suppose it has been interesting for me to take notice of how some of the poorest people I've met are on a mission to make more money. The top achievers I have learned from have been on a mission to do things in a quality way but in a shorter time span. In other words, how to create results in the least amount of time possible. The formula naturally appears that once you can do something in the shortest ration of time, you can do more of it, which leads to a result of abundance.

The average person is not as concerned with how time is spent. Often, they are not even aware of how time is gradually leaking out of their life. I have always hoped that when we die, we will be given a scorecard that gives us the actual number of hours we spent watching television (especially specific shows), how much time we spent waiting in traffic, how much time sleeping in, how much time we spend making excuses, etc. Not that this information would help us in any way, and I am probably like you in the sense that I know that whatever the number is it's going to make me feel bad. However, as I have thought about this, it's often given me some motivation to try to seal my daily time leaks and do better.

 POWER THOUGHT: Most people settle for the life they live rather than the life they want. Pay attention to the life you are choosing to live.

Exercise: Take a look at your day and identify some of your consistent time leaks. How can you use this time more productively? I have found that with each time ooze in my schedule, I have been able to trade it for something more valuable. I have felt more energized about my day and a keen sense of progress after I did this.

Happiness Exists in the Present

A few years ago, I ran across an interesting study on happiness and how it is achieved. This topic was extremely interesting to me because it correlates directly to what I share as a definition of success. Do you remember near the beginning of this book when I shared that a successful outcome is defined as a specific and a feeling?

The highest two pinnacles of that feeling are happiness and joy (they are different from each other, and that's a lesson for another book). However, as I read this 100 plus page scientific study on happiness, I recognized a reoccurring theme. Don't worry, I am not going to try to be all mathematical and methodical on you. I'm going to simply say it in my own words. More than 100 pages were summed up with this concept: *happiness is found in being present in the moment.*

You won't find much happiness longing for the past, and you won't find it in a powerful manifestation looking toward the future. **The happiest people find it in the moment.**

This is a lot harder for most people to do than you'd think. Even sitting across from someone in a conversation, you can't help but have your mind drift to something you need to prepare for later, or question whether you did something at home, or anything else other than the present.

Exercise: Think back to the last time you had a conversation with a colleague or your spouse. Where was your mind? Were you in the present moment or were you planning your next one? Oftentimes, those who think they are present usually aren't. I call this micro-planning. You may be engaged in the conversation but not necessarily planning for some distant activity. Perhaps, you're simply planning what you're going to say next. That's micro-planning. *You can't be present when you're planning.*

Becoming a top achiever does require you to plan for the future and to evaluate the past. However, one of the prime skills that top people of action have is the ability to be 100% present when their attention is required.

The good news is this: it is a talent that can be developed and begins with awareness. Naturally, the more you practice this skill, the easier it will be to develop. I believe this is one of the reasons I enjoy practicing mixed martial arts. When I am involved in a match with someone, and my mind is elsewhere instead of the immediate present, I am very quickly reminded to stay focused. I'm not suggesting that part of the PPM program is to go and start cage fighting. There are many ways you can begin to practice being in the present zone. Find something that works for you.

Fear Does Not Exist in the Present

You might find this fascinating. Generally, people do not do the things they need to in order to create success because of this: they are afraid. As I have conducted PPM events over the last two decades, I have had hundreds of people list fear as the reason for their hesitancy to create the life they really want. **Fear is powerful, but it's a very dark power that robs you of an epic life.**

Here's the good news. *If you live in the present, you won't have anything left to fear.* You see, fear doesn't exist in the present. **Fear is a condition that requires the future.** Fear only exists in the future. Fear is always based on what may happen, not necessarily what is happening at that moment. Even a fear that is based on something in the past requires the future in order to repeat that past failure or challenge. If you are present in the moment, fear has no place. If you have read the Bible, there are multiple scriptures that begin with "Fear not" or "Do not fear." That's telling!

If you don't believe me, think back to some of the most frightening things you have faced. I have had people in my events that have been in combat environments, situations where their homes have been on fire with their family inside, people who have been in serious car wrecks, and even those who were the victim of home invasions and worse. While there was a degree of fear involved, those who made it out of those situations in one piece acted without fear to escape. *As soon as they shifted from worrying about an outcome, they had the power to act at that very moment.*

Exercise: The next time you are afraid, recognize where the fear is focusing. Is it a possible future event? You'll discover that it is. With that awareness, do yourself a huge favor, draw yourself back to the present moment, and take action.

You may have additionally heard that fear stands for **F**alse **E**vidence **A**ppearing **R**eal. I like this, but the one we use in PPM is better and more effective because it is more accurate. **Fear** is **F**uture **E**vent **A**ttention **R**obbery. It is a possible future event trying to rob you of your current attention. Next time you feel fear moving into your mind, recognize it for what it is – you have a **F E A R** in progress, stop it.

Fear is a useless superstition. It is also powerful to recognize that the vast majority of the things you fear will never happen. We often assume the worst because of the defense mechanism of our mind.

 POWER THOUGHT: Amazing things cannot be created in the future or the past. You need to use the present.

The Universe Rewards Momentum

Several years ago, I had a man come up to me at one of my events and say how happy he was that I was about to motivate his team. This really concerned me as I looked at his team. They were not excited to be there, and they certainly weren't going to be easy to get motivated.

As I spoke with them, we discussed what motivation really meant, and this manager was very disappointed to see that none of his people were inspired based on our definitions.

After a few minutes talking about motivation, I asked the question about what is more powerful – motivation or momentum. Suddenly I saw the audience come alive as people began to get excited about the idea of knocking down the concepts of motivation. They didn't just want to be motivated.

 POWER THOUGHT: Motivation is temporary, and it needs to constantly be pushed to performance and action. However, momentum is different. Once people have momentum, it is easier to move forward.

As the conversation started, it took on a momentum of its own, which proved my point even further. Motivation is a hard thing to get onside with, especially if it's not your idea. Once the momentum gets going, even if it isn't your idea, it's easy to start becoming a contributor. I'll discuss more about getting momentum out of teams in a future book, but for today, let's take a look at how this looks for you personally. Remember the present!

I've had students who weren't motivated to start working out, but the minute they got moving, the momentum took over and now they do it every day.

I've had others who had challenges creating positive situations in their relationships because they had been in a rut for so long. As soon as the momentum started, they began to see positive results.

Others had great entrepreneurial ideas, but did nothing because they didn't know where to start. With a few initial tasks, more clarity appeared, and the momentum led them from step to step. **Those who choose to stop and analyze often become paralyzed.**

Find ways to create and keep momentum. It's like a heavy iron train on the tracks. Getting it going can be tough, but keeping it going is easier.

One More Thought on Momentum

This is maybe not the place in the book to share this, or maybe it is. Anyway, I'm choosing to put it here because I think it fits best here. Multiple times, I have witnessed people who have great momentum until they begin to create some of the outcomes they are excited about. In other words, as they begin to experience some success, they get comfortable and slow everything down to celebrate and enjoy the fruits of their labors.

Those who stop to enjoy their success have a very difficult time creating more. This is why I believe it is important to always revise some of the early concepts of this book. Mastery is a journey, and if you have achieved some great outcomes, then raise the bar. Never settle and recognize that if you have done something great, it is only a sign that there is more greatness within you.

Capturing the Present Requires Sacrifice

To create the life you really want, *you will have to make sacrifices.*

Change means that some things cannot stay the same. Obviously, there are some things you will gladly let go of and remove from your life. But the real challenges come when it is necessary to sacrifice things that are actually quite good to get to things that are much better, especially when that sacrifice is being made in faith.

The word sacrifice means to make sacred. Sacred means to set apart for a special purpose. When we consecrate ourselves to become more perfected and sacred, we are setting ourselves apart for a higher cause. Most people take life as it comes. They don't believe they are worthy of a higher purpose than what they currently have.

One of the hardest sacrifices I have observed most people holding back isn't money. Money is actually pretty easy for most people to part with. Time is much harder to give to someone than money. However, there is one thing even harder to give up than time: security and perfection.

Most people want to have security, understanding and perfection before they decide to trust who they can become. They don't want to make mistakes and they don't want to fail. Instead, they would rather do nothing or are determined to wait until they feel they understand a thing so well that they can't help but succeed.

 POWER THOUGHT: Momentum is easier to get than motivation. Once you experience results, you are more easily convinced to keep going than when you were only prompted by motivation.

You must be willing to make the sacrifices required to create or maintain the life you desire as those moments arrive in real time. Once the moment has passed, so has the opportunity.

Sacrifice Can Also be Seen in Our Priorities and Focus

Most people struggle with trying to discover their priorities. They often focus on the wrong things that do not produce the results they are ultimately looking for. *Focus is really an exercise in management.* Most people spend a great deal of time trying to manage their life, manage their time and manage the tasks that they are faced with.

Management is really an act of determining what is most important to you and what you can sacrifice to make those important things happen. If your primary effort is focus on management, you will experience difficulty, stress and failure.

As I have taught company leaders and managers around the world (people regularly get these two titles confused), *a manager and a leader are not the same things.* Moreover, if we can understand the difference, the insight will translate to more power in our personal lives as well.

Leadership Must Proceed Management

Management is the sorting of tasks to be done. Leadership is recognizing which tasks are important.

When you understand from the previous chapters about what outcomes you really want and how those choices resonate with your truest values, you are a leader. You are in charge of the outcomes you are attempting to create.

Once you are a leader, you can recognize what tasks need to be included in your efforts and which ones are not supporting you. You can manage and focus on what will be of most value to you in your life.

The Funnel Effect

One of the most profound moments in my visits with the world's top dynamos was when I learned about a principle called the funnel effect. Just this idea alone will make a significant difference in reaching the outcomes and successes you are attempting to create in your life.

Here's how it was explained to me:

Most people live their life like a funnel. At the top of the funnel is a wide mouth and then it flows down to the narrow spout.

We can compare the wide entrance to the funnel to how most people live their lives. If they want more money, they put in more hours. If they want bigger businesses, they feel the answer is to meet with more clients or increase their marketing techniques and outreaches. If they want a more enjoyable life, they feel like they need more. If they want to connect better with people, they try to give more. Everything is about more, and following the flow of the funnel, they ultimately get less – just like the narrow spout at the bottom.

Risk takers and individuals of action actually do things quite differently. Instead of using the funnel the way most people perceive it, they flip it upside down. Instead of serving more and trying to do more, they actually attempt to do less but in a sharpened way. **They focus on quality over quantity.**

As they establish boundaries and make sacrifices, they become greater on a very focused and specific set of things rather than trying to be all things to everyone. By doing less, but in higher quality, they ultimately obtain much more.

It reminds me of what Napoleon Hill said in his book *Think and Grow Rich*. **The riches are in the niches.**

One way I explain this in my PPM events contradicts a lot of what you've been verbally fed by many of the self-help gurus of today. I may even stir up some controversy in saying this but what the heck. Let's do it!

The gurus of today are frequently quoted as telling you that your greatest progress will occur as you step outside of your comfort zone. I'm here right now to tell you that is not true. As I observed more than 400 of the world's top achievers, (I want to remind you again of the sheer volume of 400 people), this was a common link with all of them, not just a few. They did not endeavor to step outside their comfort zone and get into areas of their weaknesses. Instead, they sought to stay in their areas of strength. I call it the **brilliance zone.**

These top achievers attempted to stay in their brilliance zone. They stayed close to what they were good at, and if they needed support in their weak areas, they sought help and delegated to those who were specifically brilliant where they weren't as strong.

Now I want to point out something here so that I am not misunderstood. These top achievers did stretch and push themselves into areas of their lives that were uncomfortable, but they only got uncomfortable with a purpose and within their brilliance zone.

Using the Present is an Essential Key

I want to conclude this chapter by reminding you how crucial it is to stay in the present moment. The word "now," in my opinion, is the most fragile word in the English language. Once you say it, it is gone forever, *and what you experience in the present can never be brought back*. It is gone forever.

As I interviewed the top movers and shakers in the world, this perception became alarmingly clear. There were countless times when I had just a few brief moments to connect with some of the top achievers whom I interviewed. In fact, had I not taken the steps to start a conversation with some as I ran into them in a rush, I would have never had a second chance to have those dialogs.

Opportunity is like a lightning strike. You pretty much don't know when it will happen, or if it will happen again. If you miss it, you will never get a second chance. Our lives are not like what happened to Michael J. Fox in the movie *Back to the Future*. Real life is full of uncertainties, and will continue to be.

When an opportunity presents itself, you won't have the time to think about it. You have to know what you want ahead of time and be prepared to take immediate action.

Questions on the Power of the Present to Consider:

1. What can you do to decrease the amount of time you need to create results without sacrificing quality?

2. How are you allowing fear to take you out of the present moment?

3. Where are you losing time without a return on your investment?

4. How are you sealing your time leaks?

5. What sacrifices will you have to make?

6. How can you create more momentum?

7. What are you hanging on to that is good, but prevents you from getting to things that are better?

8. How can you be more present?

9. How are you showing the universe you are hesitant?

10. Are you a leader or a manager?

11. How is the funnel effect appearing in your life?

12. What is your brilliance zone?

13. Whom can you delegate your weaknesses to?

CHAPTER EIGHT

The Power of
Deliberate Activity

*The most difficult thing is the decision to
act. The rest is merely tenacity.*

- Amelia Earhart

To perform externally, we must align internally

Focus on the outcomes most likely to occur

**Hesitation tells the universe that you
are not ready to receive**

I decided it was very important to add the word "deliberate" to the title of this chapter. One of the reasons why is because of a quote that you often hear that really bugs me. You've heard it too and it goes like this, "The journey of 1,000 miles begins with a single footstep."

Quite frankly, there are a few things about this quote that just rub me the wrong way. The first thing is it sounds like you're beginning a journey where you're going to be lost in the desert for 1,000 miles. I don't like that idea.

I also feel that the idea of a single footstep makes it sound like it's going to be a slow go and will take a long time to get there.

If I were to rewrite that quote, I would prefer it to say, "The journey to where you want to get to begins with a *single leap* in the right direction."

Deliberate activities are calculated to take you in a specific direction. I think most people need 1,000 miles because they really don't know where they are going or what outcomes they would like to create. Since we've discussed destination earlier, I don't think there is a need to do that again. But now the activity you engage in is a monumental subject.

Most people wait for everything to be perfect before they get moving. Many people also follow an incorrect pattern of action. Sometimes they call it goal setting. Most of what is taught today in establishing goals is not correct, and I didn't see it in my research of the 400 top achievers.

I would like to share what they did to achieve their outcomes and accelerate your abilities to take leaps instead of steps.

Why Goal Setting Doesn't Work

The way top achievers approach the accomplishment of their outcomes is not new. In fact, I discovered where our current system for goal achievement and goal setting came from after thorough research.

I really wish I had been able to discover the title and author of the book when I was in an antique bookstore in Utah several years ago. I was talking with the store owner about my interviews with the top achievers and the concepts of goal setting. He immediately lit up and told me there was something I needed to see. He hurried to the back and found an old book missing the cover and nearly half of its pages. The book was yellowed and full of worn pages. The store owner believed the book was written in the early 1800s and passed it across to me. As I looked through it, I was surprised to skim quickly through and find that a lot of the content was very similar to many of the self-help books of our day. There was a chapter on belief, one on taking action, and one specifically on goal setting.

As I asked the store owner about this publication, he told me that he believed it was probably the first North American self-help book ever printed. He believed that it was most likely the influence for everything that had come out since. He also informed me that I was welcome to take some time and read it a bit.

At the time, I was most intrigued by goal setting, so that's what I chose to read about. As I studied what was in front of me, I instantly saw how this book had influenced the way planning your goals is looked at today. I could also see that it was wrong.

The book stated that people are like assembly lines (just that alone should let you know we are off track). And if a person wanted X number of units as the outcome, they simply needed to work backward. They should list and complete all of the jobs on the assembly line that would give you the desired number of units at the conclusion or whatever else you might be looking to create. I guess you could say what that author was teaching was the idea of reverse engineering.

There are two major problems with this, however. *The first is that we are human beings, not human doings.* By focusing only on the tasks to be completed it, is very difficult for most people to stay motivated and inspired to keep going. Perhaps this is why so many people set New Year's resolutions (losing weight is a big one) and fail or set business goals and fail. They're solely based on logic.

If a person is going to achieve greatness in his/her outcomes, they must come from something bigger than logic. Remember how in an earlier chapter I talked about the foundation of specifics and feelings. In order to take action again and again, especially when it is difficult, we must involve our feelings.

Our feelings and our values determine who we are and what we are ultimately most committed to. We always return to doing what we value most. This is why most people can't stay focused on the goals they say matter most to them because they actually don't share the same feeling about them.

We must become aligned internally before we can perform externally in order to create the outcome we say we want. Be, then do, then have.

My wife once put it this way, which I think is a powerful observation: *"You've heard that actions speak louder than words, but being speaks louder than acting. When we are the right thing, we do the right thing, and we get to have the right thing."*

The second problem with the assembly line manufacturing idea is this next concept that trips most people up. *Time.* To complete all the jobs on the assembly line simply takes too much time.

Top achievers never try to do all the jobs laid before them. In fact, delegation, leverage and support, which we will talk about in the next chapter, are some of their greatest tools.

 **POWER THOUGHT: We only act on the ideas that are emotionally charged for us.
If it means nothing, we do nothing.**

The Law of Probability

The way in which we act is called the law of probability. Aristotle once stated, "That which is probable is most likely to happen." It sounds basic, but it's true. Rather than creating a checklist of things to complete, the law of probability focuses on what you can do to make the outcomes most likely to occur.

Let me use an example. If there were a target at the far side of a 100-yard field, what would be the chances that you could fire an arrow directly into the center of it? For most people, it would be very unlikely.

What would happen to your chances if you took a step toward the target? Naturally, they would increase. What if you took another step forward? They would expand again.

This is the law of probability. It is finding ways to take steps closer and closer to your target until the chances that you will achieve your outcome are secured.

There are essentially four ways you will increase the probability of your desired result:

1. **People**: The people you meet and surround yourself with can open doors, inspire, support and even work for you to help increase the probability that you will get to your outcome. In the next chapter, I am going to talk more about support and relationships to create outcomes, but for now, I want to share a theory called 6-degrees of separation. The theory suggested that we are separated from every other person on the planet by six other people; thus, 6-degrees of separation.

   I don't believe it exists like that anymore. Instead, I am convinced that with the way social media is today, you are often separated from everyone on the globe by between zero and two people. You can literally get to anyone. If we had time, I could tell you at least 200 stories about how I was put in contact with some of the top achievers in my interviews. It would literally astound you.

2. **Knowledge**: What you know is a powerful way to increase the probability that your outcome will occur. *The more you know, the more power you have to make powerful choices.* You'll remember the quote I shared at the beginning of this chapter regarding the journey to where you want to go begins with a leap in the right direction. When you obtain awareness and expertise, you can move faster and make fewer mistakes.

3. **Geography**: Today, when many people are content to work from behind a laptop in a hidden corner of their home or a coffee shop somewhere, I am still of the opinion that getting out of those environments can increase your probability in massive ways. There are some locations that are just better for creating your outcomes. For example, several of my top achievers were either musicians or actors. Both of those categories agreed that if you wanted to be in movies, your chances were better in Los Angeles than Moosejaw Saskatchewan.

   You've also heard of people who achieved their success because they were supposedly in the right place at the right time. Well,

I do believe there is truth to that, and the more time you spend in the right place, the more likely it is that you will meet people that can help you and gain knowledge that will open doors. Just like in the real estate profession – *think location, location, location.*

4. **Frequency:** The fourth principle of increasing your probability is frequency. The more frequently you meet the right people, learn the right things and go to the right locations, the more your probability will increase. Let me emphasize that it is not enough to meet someone once or learn something once, or even go to the right location once. **You need to do it repeatedly.** It needs to become part of your pattern.

 POWER THOUGHT: An Olympic athlete does not stop at one gold medal. Nor does he or she only train once a day to win that medal. Consistency and persistence are key.

Opportunities Appear in Activity

Often when I am teaching PPM, it is not uncommon for some participants to say that they would be happy to take action once an opportunity appears. They hold back waiting for a big sign from the sky or someone to draw them a map. The universe will draw you a map, but it generally waits until your feet are moving before guiding them.

As you step into the unknown, start with what you can do instead of searching for what you could do if the path were revealed to you beforehand.

The Universe Takes Its Cues From You

As I have had many opportunities to genuinely get to know the teachers in the movie *The Secret* (either as they've appeared in my movies or as I've shared the stage with them around the world), it has been interesting to observe that they are all go-getters. As I spoke with Bob Doyle once about this aspect of the law of attraction, he said something very poignant to me: *"When people hesitate to take immediate action, they are teaching the universe they are not immediately ready to receive. Approach something with hesitation, it will arrive with hesitation."*

If you are clear about what you want, it is crucial that you act boldly and directly as it arrives. If we hesitate, it is a reflection of the level of commitment that we feel. Our feelings as you are discovering are directly attached to the outcomes that we experience.

You Won't Always Be Perfect

Obviously, as you go out into the world and get to work on your dreams, there will be a learning curve. Sometimes this learning may be very public. I wish I could have seen that everything I attempted to do worked out smoothly. I have made mistakes – public mistakes – and it sucks, believe me, but it is important to recognize that top achievers are not perfectionists, they are improvisers.

In education, there is a term called the J curve. You may remember this from the chapter on change, but I wanted to stress it here again with a real-life example. This is how everything is learned. If you think about the shape of the J, everyone starts at the beginning of the small hook.

Let's say you are learning how to ride a bike. You would begin and immediately discover what knowledge you lack. You would descend the J, and those bumps and bruises would appear as you lost balance and fell. However, as you continue, you would slowly gain mastery (there's an interesting word), and you would develop balance, speed and competence while riding your bike.

As you came around the curve at the back of the J, things would get easier and less complicated until you started to ascend the back stem of the J and go higher in your skill level than ever before. Ultimately, one day you would have the ability to even ride your bike while holding a soft drink in one hand and your phone in the other. Heck, you might even choose to go no-hands!

Everything is learned this way. It's important that you have correct expectations that there will be a learning curve, you will experience failures and setbacks, and everything won't turn out perfect on the first try.

One of the things that I observed as a powerful strength that nearly all of the top achievers had was that they didn't let failure or adversity trouble them for long. They learned what they could, picked themselves up and kept going.

Each time they picked themselves up they became a different person. Remember what we said about be, do and then have. *They were becoming someone greater than they were before.*

Expand who you are, and you get to expand what you have. This is the mathematics of success.

 POWER THOUGHT: Top achievers are improvisers, not perfectionists. If you want to create more success in your life, you have to move forward not knowing all the answers.

Stupidity Versus Persistence

When I was a young man beginning these interviews with the world's top achievers, one of my relatives made a comment that really bothered me and, in fact, almost stopped my mission. As I reached out to some of the top achievers for a visit, I often received rejections or was handed off to someone else. It was often very difficult to get to some of the people I wanted to meet with. One of my relatives, upon hearing of my mission said, "When are you going to understand there is a difference between stupidity and tenacity? Right now, you're being stupid."

I'll be honest, I didn't think I was stupid, and I kept going. Ultimately it paid off, but as I have taught PPM over the years, I have seen many people who were accused of being stupid instead of tenacious (often it came from a family member). So, what's the difference?

This is a question that I have spent a lot of time thinking about. Here is my answer:

Stupidity is banging your head against a wall to get into the other room. *Tenacity is trying new strategies until you find the door that will take you into the other room.*

Stubborn and stupid are always afraid to be shown that they are wrong. They will use the same method again and again without progress. They are unteachable, and eventually, they will die still banging their head against the same wall.

Persistence and tenacity are confident in an outcome and are willing to learn from others and adjust their strategy.

Don't be afraid to fail. Be afraid to be stupid and stubborn.

Robert was at one of my events a few years ago. His wife was quite frustrated because he had been trying to make a business work for years while he was working at a second full-time job. No matter what he tried, the business just wasn't taking off, and people weren't seeming that interested in what he was doing. He knew, though, that he had a winner idea and was not about to give up.

Robert had been to multiple seminars and had every book, CD and program that encouraged him to continue rather than kill his dreams. He was being tenacious.

When he came to my PPM event, we talked about his goal of owning a successful business. He felt validated and renewed his commitment to making his business a success. He was excited and delighted. But looking at his wife, she had been through this before and was not impressed.

She spoke of how things were not currently working, and every month this meant more money and heightened frustrations. She was at her wit's end and didn't know what she could do next.

It was then that we discussed the difference between tenacity and stupidity. This made sense to both of them, and Robert was very happy to recognize that the dream or outcome is rarely stupid. The stupidity is found in the approach or the method to get there. I gave them the following exercise, which I would like to give to you now.

Exercise: Consider something you have been trying for a long time and have had difficulty achieving success with. Remember that the dream is rarely stupid, but often the methods or the approach may be. Make a list of the approaches that you have taken and what the outcome was.

Return now to the very beginning of this book where we talked about choices. What alternative strategies could you try that might help you attain your desired outcomes and results?

You've probably heard the idea that Thomas Edison had more than 10,000 attempts before he was successful at creating the light bulb. That may or may not have been true. But even if he tried 100 times, I am confident that each of those times was different. How many diverse methods have you tried?

Let's be honest when people say they've tried a million times, what they generally mean is that they tried once or twice but wound up quitting. Give it a real try, and you'll eventually find undeniable results.

Questions on Deliberate Action to Consider:

1. How can you use the law of probability in your life?

2. How can you meet the right people?

3. How can you learn the right things?

4. How can you spend more time in the right places?

5. How can you get momentum?

6. How will you keep the momentum going?

7. Are you willing to learn in the J curve?

8. Do you have correct expectations that failure will occur?

9. Are you committed enough to keep going?

10. Are you being tenacious or stupid?

11. How many times have you really tried?

12. Are you willing to try again right now?

13. What other options are there?

CHAPTER NINE

The Power of Support

Accepting help is its own
kind of strength.

- Kiera Cass

Great work is achieved by people working together

Your problems do not always need to be solved by you

You don't need all the answers. You need others who do

The first time that I stood on the Great Wall of China I was in awe, but not for the reason that you might think.

I stood on the Great Wall surrounded by bustling tourists with cameras. There was commotion all around me as people pointed out how remarkable the wall was snaking over the hillside for miles in each direction. People had told me that the Great Wall was visible from outer space, and standing on it, I believed it was possible. The wall is just that large.

While everyone was focused on how far and long the wall reached out, I paused and looked down at my feet.

Something really impressed me and got me thinking. As I looked down, I couldn't help but see that the Great Wall was composed of tiny bricks. Honestly, in my head, I said the Great Wall is made of small bricks that aren't really that great at all.

As I reflected on my realization, I thought about how the important things in our lives are built the same way. It is the small and apparently average-looking things that come together to build the things in our lives that are truly great.

In addition, I thought about how each brick supported the other in a way to synergistically create such a massive structure. Our lives require the same to create bigger and better outcomes. If you look at the entire history of the world, the greatest things ever achieved in the history of mankind were accomplished not by individuals, but by groups of people working together to make big things happen.

For example, Sir Edmund Hillary received credit for being the first person to climb Mount Everest; however, people forget he had guides and Sherpas who carried equipment and provided expert advice.

Neil Armstrong may have been the first man on the Moon, but he had an entire team back in Texas and Florida who had designed the rocket and the lunar capsule which arrived and returned home safely.

Even a solo artist like Elvis Presley had Colonel Parker, a record company, fans who bought records and much more that made him successful. **Everyone needs a support team.**

Support comes in a few ways, and I am going to talk about a few of the support elements in this chapter.

 POWER THOUGHT: If you are serious about your success you need to seek out the best in everything to help you get there.

People

We have already talked a little bit about the importance of people when I introduced the law of probability. Yet, I feel people are such an important part of great success that we need to revisit this.

You've heard the saying that *your net worth is equal to your network.* This would suggest that your income is a reflection of those you spend the most time with. I have seen this maxim verified many times.

However, what I am talking about here doesn't just apply to finances. My friend Randy Gage pointed out that it also applies to relationships, which was demonstrated in my movie called *The*

Treasure Map. Your marriage will reflect the other couples you spend time with. Additionally, your health will reflect those you spend time with and so forth.

Who you deliberately choose to admire and spend time with will show up in your life.

I want to also indicate something we share in PPM, which is that *network* is two words.

Net represents your safety zone. Those who you spend time with in your network equip your source of solving personal and professional life difficulties. As you level up, your network shapes your ability to solve more complex problems in your life and for your business to grow as well.

Exercise: Consider what challenges or obstacles you're currently experiencing in your life. Who in your network could be a support or an asset in helping you discover or create a solution? Who could you ask for help? Furthermore, what kind of help could they give you?

Albert Einstein once said that "a problem is never solved at the same level of thinking that created it." I want to add that a problem doesn't always have to be solved by the same person who created it as well. Get help from your network, especially if something seems too big for you to deal with.

Having a dream team or a team supreme helping you with problematic questions and even easy questions is the way top achievers operate.

Several years ago, I was sitting in the home of Bill Farley. At one point, Bill was the CEO of Fruit of the Loom underwear. As we sat in his house, we started talking about a business idea. Without hesitation, he took the phone beside him and, almost instantly, an entire team of people came into the room. He explained the business idea to the group, and they each, in turn, gave their points of view. He nodded and then dismissed them. After considering their opinion, he told me his decision.

It was impressive to watch how he used his network to immediately help him answer questions in real time.

The other part of that word network is **work**. Work indicates that high-level relationships don't just happen; there is a degree of work that needs to be committed to make things happen.

Overall, I would prefer to take the idea that your network is equivalent to your net worth and rewrite it as this: your network actually equals your self-worth, and everything follows from that.

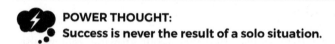

POWER THOUGHT:
Success is never the result of a solo situation.

One of my success interviews and longtime friend Darren Jacklin said to me once, "If you hang out with four losers, you are destined to become the fifth." Darren is an example of someone who is influenced by those he hangs out with. He is the co-founder of Solaris Resort & Estates and private islands.

Our peers influence our behavior much more than we think. When we were teenagers, we were often warned about the dangers of peer pressure. The thing that our teachers and parents forgot to mention is that peers can have a positive influence on us too.

In fact, most of the time those we are with can give us power and strength to overcome fear, hesitation and doubt. When our friends think big, it is easier for us to think big. When our friends believe something is possible, we begin to look at possibilities too. Notice the pattern?

I have also observed that most times people will do more for others than they will for themselves. As an example, look at a lot of mothers. They often put their children first and themselves last. They try with all their might to take care of others and often, in the end, have very little time or energy to take care of themselves. This tendency appears in many areas of our lives.

Obviously, you do need to take care of yourself, and you can't rely on others as your source of motivation. The name of this book is *Personal Power Mastery*, but it is important that we consider that other people can be a massive source of motivation throughout the process.

As far as people go, I want to spend some time talking about the principle of leverage. As I spoke with most of the top achievers, the topic of leverage was something that became a conversation point almost instantly.

You also hear that people often talk about growing your wealth or your business through the support of other people's money, sometimes referred to as OPM.

There are other things you can leverage as well. Let me share what I call the big four:

Money: To go into more detail on this concept, Felix Dennis ranked for many years on *The Sunday Times* Rich List Top 100 of Britain's Wealthiest Individuals, stated in regards to money, "You can be given it or inherit it; you can win it; you can steal it; you can marry it; you can earn it; you can borrow it." *All of those ways to have money come into your life involve other people.* If you want to have other people's money come into your life in an honest way to help you get to your dreams, only one of those answers is unsuccessful.

Money from other people can be available for you to grow your business and your life. More on this in a moment.

Time: Time is the most unappreciated asset that we have in this life. Hear this: **time is the one thing we can never duplicate or create more of!** Once it is gone, it's gone. As I interviewed the top achievers, it was interesting to note that most of them spoke about ways to save time, free up and manage time far more than they ever spoke of money. Perhaps this is a clue if one of the outcomes you are looking to create is more abundance. One of my achievers stated it this way, "Learning how to manage your time comes before learning how to manage your money. When you figure out how to effectively use your time and grow it, money will follow."

You cause the time of others to free up and multiply your time. More on this in a moment too.

Knowledge: You don't have to have all of the answers, but you need to know those who do. One of the stories that has always stayed with me from *Think and Grow Rich* was the story of Henry Ford. He was once involved in a defamation of character lawsuit, which involved the *Chicago Tribune* calling him ignorant. Rather than apologize, the newspaper set out to prove he was ignorant in a court of law.

During the court proceedings, the opposition lawyers tried to confound Henry Ford and asked him all kinds of historical questions. Finally, after trying to deal with his contenders, Ford simply said, "I have a row of electric push-buttons on my desk, and by pushing the right button, I can summon to my aid men who can answer *any* question I desire to ask concerning the business to which I am devoting most of my efforts. Now, will you kindly tell me WHY I should clutter up my mind with general knowledge, for the purpose of being able to answer questions, when I have men around me who can supply any knowledge I require?"

More on this in a moment.

Authority: This is one that most people don't consider, but it is everywhere, and what I believe is one of the fastest ways to help you achieve your outcomes. A great example of this can be seen on television in the form of celebrity endorsements or testimonials in a book. I experienced it first-hand with my first movie, *The Opus*. I was able to exponentially grow my career through my association with those I had chosen for our movie.

You can never leverage the assets, time, knowledge or authority of another person until you have learned how to manage these things first in yourself. In other words, no one will give you money until they believe that you can manage your own money properly. No one will give you their time, or at least you won't be able to properly benefit from their time, until you can use your own effectively. The same goes for knowledge and especially for authority. After all, who would loan their name to someone with a bad reputation?

In the principle of leverage, you are the first one that needs to demonstrate a comprehension of the principle by what you do with yourself.

Are You a Taker or a Giver?

In addition to knowing that you need help, you must understand why others might choose to help you. In order to make yourself helpful, you need to understand how you can be of assistance to others. As I interviewed the top achievers around the world, one common attribute that I found was that they were genuine givers and supportive people. They wanted to help others succeed, but they were also aware of takers.

Givers have a warm and kind energy, while takers exude the opposite. Eventually, that particular energy will be very obvious to even the most helpful of people. Consequently, they will stop supporting takers. You may not have something that you can immediately contribute back to some of the mentors or supporters who are ready to help you. However, even if you don't have something in the present moment, a true giver will sense that you have the giving energy. They will continue to help as long as they feel that energy, and that you are attempting to edify them and support others.

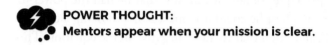

POWER THOUGHT:
Mentors appear when your mission is clear.

Relationships

Support from people first appears in the relationships we seek out and nurture. I say seek out even when I am speaking about parents, siblings, significant others and children. Just because a relationship is by blood doesn't mean that it is one we cherish and nurture. It is a regular occurrence in PPM to encounter someone attending the training with a specific goal to improve a relationship in this immediate circle of family.

Phil was married with three children. The children are all in school now and a little older. He recognized that his relationship with his wife had been in trouble for years, yet they hid it behind a desire to protect the children. With them spending less time at home, the troubles began to be more obvious and harder to deal with.

Phil arrived at PPM by himself for the first time. He was so inspired by the power he recognized within himself to change things in his life, he set out on a mission to reconnect with his wife. At the event, I shared with him a simple principle called the relationship equation. In the equation, the number 1 represents you and the person you are in a relationship with. Together in the equation, you both create an outcome that could be expressed like this: $1 + 1 = 2$

Most people point blame at the other partner in the equation and spend all their energy and effort trying to get the other person to change. As a result, both partners dig in and remain the same in the equation, and the outcome stays the same. Think of the recovery programs that are out there – they are focused on changing yourself instead of trying to force others to change. This shift has brought peace and serenity into their lives and, oftentimes, relationships.

The simple principle we taught Phil was that he had the power to either come out a 0 or he could become a 2 or a 3. Being a 0 is not helpful at all, and often that creates a negative in the equation. The latter would cause the outcome of the equation to be a 3 or 4. And the change would happen regardless of the thoughts or actions of his partner.

I taught him how to anchor himself to the concept of creating a 3 or a 4, and he eagerly got to work. In a relatively short period of time, those in his family began to notice changes within Phil.

The next PPM that took place in his city, I met Phil's wife. She also learned of this concept, and together they are creating 4, 5 and 6 results. Sometimes when one of them slumps back into a 1 as their part of the equation, the other recognizes it and helps shift to make up the difference. Things aren't always perfect, but they have their power back.

Employees, Teams and Associates

This is another category where people form an important part of creating outcomes. Sometimes these people are either employees or are working alongside you. These kinds of relationships benefit most when communication is clear and win/win synergy is created. Studies have demonstrated that employers may buy the employees' time, but loyalty is a separate issue. *Loyalty includes diligent efforts, best ideas and enthusiastic contribution.*

One of the principles we teach in PPM for teams and managers unfolds the idea that leadership is more important methodology. Sharing outcomes should always allow for individuals to discover and determine their attachment and approach to creating the desired outcomes.

Let's return to the idea of how supportive people in this category are peers who will influence your performance in your work or business.

Mentors and Coaches

I consider most of the top achievers who taught me over the years as mentors in my life. Most of them have become lifelong friends and teachers that I still learn from today. Many of them attend PPM as supports to my students the same way they were to me.

I really appreciate what one of my friends, Joseph McClendon III, had to say about the difference between mentors and coaches. **Mentors are those who have been there versus the ones who only have an outside perspective.** Mentors are the fastest way to create the outcomes you want.

A Warning

Before I move on to the other aspects of support and influence, I want to share a warning. I only share this because I've seen how destructive the next topic can be and how this challenge can interfere with creating success and positive outcomes. The thing I want to warn about is scarcity thinking when it comes to other people.

You can't have one foot in scarcity and attract abundance.

Scarce thinking most often manifests itself in jealousy, criticism and comparison.

Jealousy is a negative emotion, and it keeps you from focusing on what you can do to improve your situation. It's a thief of your energy. There is an old saying that you can't reach up while you're holding something else (or someone else) down. Jealousy is an anchor that keeps you from climbing higher. Jealousy has never created anything wonderful. You don't need it to become better.

Criticism is a manifestation of jealousy. Criticism is dangerous because you can never attract what you criticize. If you are looking to create good relationships at home, but you criticize your partner, or the apparent success others are having, you can never draw that into your own life.

If you are trying to create more financial abundance but are constantly criticizing others who are financially successful, you will never attract wealth into your life.

Each of these activities separates you from connecting with people and the energy of expansion and growth.

A final way that people slow their progress and separate themselves from others is through comparison. Comparison is a form of competition. The only challenge is that you are never competing in a way that you could possibly win. When you compare your life or achievements to others, you forget that they are actually playing by a different set of rules. Often their goals, values or intentions have very little resemblance to yours. You are comparing yourself to someone who isn't even playing the same game as you. There is a slogan from those recovery support groups mentioned earlier that says, "Identify, don't compare." Everyone has a unique story to share.

Rather than compare, seek for ways to cooperate.

As you bring positive energy into your interactions with others, you will feel that spirit of the giver that I spoke about earlier begin to appear. It was fascinating for me to see that as I spent time with the top achievers, they were always excited at my successes and of those around them. They were never competitive in an attempt to one-up people around them.

Have you ever been in a situation where you are talking about a topic (it doesn't even have to be an accomplishment), and the other person goes, "Oh, I can top that!" Or "I have one even better to share!" Individuals who praise others' victories never have to jump on top of someone else's story with their stuff when someone else shared what they were doing.

Exercise: Try this the next time someone shares with you something they are doing in their life or something they achieved. Rather than search for something you can share that also makes you sound great, bite your tongue. Don't share your piece. Simply say congratulations and let them shine.

 POWER THOUGHT: There are people who feel that they have no power unless they are taking power away from others. This is a symptom of a scarcity mindset. Celebrate the successes of others.

You'll find that saying thank you and showing appreciation for other people often opens doors.

Earlier today, I was on a radio interview with my friend Kim Carson. I have gotten to know her over the course of many interviews over the years. Once the interview was finished, we continued to chat.

The conversation focused on the exciting people she had interviewed throughout her career and all of the exciting people I had interviewed. As the conversation continued, the discussion shifted. We brought up how some of the world-famous people that both of us had interviewed had actually become our personal friends and even continued the relationship far beyond the interview. As we spoke with each other, we looked at times when this happened and other times that it didn't.

Kim and I agreed that those who we continued relationships with essentially came down to being authentically and genuinely interested in the lives (not just the accomplishments) of the top achievers and not having a hidden "taker-style" agenda.

Top achievers are human too, and when you are real and see them as people, they are more inclined to be supportive and helpful even to the point of becoming a friend. Isn't that what we all want anyway?

Support for you and your mission doesn't just appear in the people you chose to surround yourself with and request support from; rather, you are influenced by everything in your environment.

Here are some of the aspects that I believe will influence and support you on your journey to success.

Waking up early: What time you wake up in the morning is a significant factor in determining the kind of day you will have. When you sleep in and start slow, the rest of the day moves lazily along, and it turns into a game of catch up.

Personally, I don't even like my alarm clock to be my boss. I try to get up every day before it goes off, and I am getting good at it.

When I wake up earlier than the others in my house, I feel a greater sense of control and proactivity. I set the boundaries around how my day will go. When I wake up earlier, I am able to get a lot done before most people are even out of bed.

One of my friends told me that waking up earlier was the only way he was able to write. So far, he has written more than a dozen books, and they have changed his financial situation and life incredibly.

In addition to waking up early, I am going to suggest your day begins with making your bed. I once read a report on the habits of the Navy Seals. For those who don't know, the Navy Seals are a special-forces branch in the military known for their high standards of excellence. One of their habits every morning is to make their beds. In the article, the Navy Seal that was being interviewed reported that making your bed is essentially starting the day with your first accomplishment. *Beginning the day productive and organized sets the pace for the balance of the day.*

Your first task: I ask my students what they do first when they wake up. Most of them answer that they check their email. I am going to encourage you not to do that. The reason why is because your email is typically filled with questions you need to answer, tasks you need to do, people that you need to respond to and a variety of other requests. This immediately puts you into a reactive state. Reactive is not how you want to start out your day, especially before your morning coffee.

Instead, be proactive on how your day will begin. I like to begin by reading, working out and taking time out to think about the things that I want. I make my decisions carefully, and that is being proactive.

Once I have established the energy and pace of my day, then I am able to let someone else interrupt it with external requests. Remember that you don't want to allow someone else's emergency to become your fire.

 POWER THOUGHT: Start your day taking care of you!! Include proactivity as part of your daily workout.

Your mind: What you put into your mind has a massive effect on the direction and results that will appear in your life. My friend Teri once shared a thought that has stuck with me for quite some time. She is a neuroscientist, so these thoughts have a little more weight than just a passing comment.

"You've heard of the abbreviation GI=GO which stands for Good In = Good Out." Teri pointed to her brain and said, "That's actually not how it works for your mind. Good In, Good Stays." Or, GIGS.

She further explained that this is the truth with negative influences as well. Bad In = Bad Stays. Or, BIBS.

Think of it this way. When you book a gig (book signing, open mic, band), it is something positive. Gigs bring in fun, festivity, and just overall good vibes. Bibs, on the other hand, are typically used for baby seepage, and it smells and looks nasty. Do you want to book a fun gig or wear a foul bib?

As I observed and interviewed the world's top achievers, I couldn't help but notice that they are very selective as to what they allow to influence them. They are very deliberate in their choices of where they spend their time and the ideas they will allow into their thinking.

I was recently talking with a psychologist friend of mine about this concept, and he was quick to point out that everything we interact with, especially the things we deliberately choose, often has a long-lasting effect. While it is true that some influences and the context in which we experience them may have a more profound effect, he felt that everything we have as an influence leaves some kind of footprint. It is a very long time for some influences to lose their potency in our mind and life.

What we bring into our mind becomes a reflection of who we will become and how we think. In his book *The Brain that Changes Itself*, Dr. Norman Doidge explores the effects that exposure to pornography has on the brain and ultimately activity. In addition to recognizing pornography as an addiction, he pointed out that exposure to pornography changes the brain and ultimately has a disturbing effect on the patterns of sexual excitement, intimacy, relationships and sexual potency.

I will also point out that pornography, drugs and gambling were not among the habits that I observed among the top achievers. Again, what we bring into our brain stays and shapes who we will become. And some of the negative changes can take time to repair.

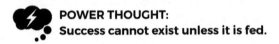 **POWER THOUGHT:**
Success cannot exist unless it is fed.

What you bring into your life: What you bring into your life also dictates the quality of life you get to experience. The top achievers in my study were very careful about committing and engaging in activities that were not in line with their major purposes. They wound up responding no more often than they said yes. They were very careful not to clutter their lives with things that did not add value to them.

One of the things that impressed me, again and again, was the order they brought into their lives and homes. They seemed to always place a high value on being organized and uncluttered.

If you want to create more success in your life, you have no choice but to deliberately seek out ways to feed and influence yourself toward higher things. This is no different than feeding your physical body with healthy food if you want optimum health. Seek out ways to spend your time (which is your most valuable and irreplaceable asset) in ways that will strengthen you and lead you closer to your great dreams. The opposite side of this equation is that you are always feeding something in your life. If it is not success, what are you creating with your time?

Consider what you are bringing into your life that influences you. What is bringing out the best in you, and what is simply taking up space? Remember, everything is a choice, and to get to the best, you may have to sacrifice some things that are good.

Questions on the Power of Support to Consider:

1. Who is in your current network?

2. How are they supporting you?

3. How are you supporting them?

4. In what ways are you using them as a safety net?

5. What will you do to level up your network?

6. How are you receiving support in your life?

7. Who is supporting you in your life?

8. How are they doing it?

9. Do you have a team that can help you make better decisions?

10. Who could you start bringing in to help?

11. Who would you like to start supporting you in your life?

12. Why would those people want to support you?

13. Are you a giver or a taker?

14. How can you have "giver energy" even when you don't have something to contribute?

15. Can you use the relationship equation?

16. How are you working with those at work?

17. Do you have a mentor or coach to help you?

18. Are you letting jealousy, criticism or comparison enter into your thinking and actions?

19. How are you celebrating the successes of others?

20. What time do you wake up?

21. What do you do when you wake up?

22. What do you put into your mind?

23. What do you bring into your life?

24. What good things can you trade for better?

CHAPTER TEN

The Power of Gratitude

*The more you use gratitude every day,
the greater the good you will bring
into your life. It is all you have to do to
completely transform your life in every
single area, and on every single subject.*

- Rhonda Byrne

Gratitude expands everything it touches

Gratitude is the highest manifestation of love

Gratitude will open doors and keep them open

As I conducted my first-hand research into the lives of more than 400 of the world's top achievers, I was also reading as many success books as possible. For those of you who follow me on Facebook, you'll see that I am still an avid reader and post a photo of all the books I read each month. On average, I read about 15-20 books a month. I blame my reading addiction on a few personal facts: I am an avid learner, I don't watch much television, and I travel a lot.

The bulk of the success interviews I did took nearly 10 years. That's almost 120 months. Over the course of time, when I was meeting the top achievers, I estimate that I read more than 2,200 books (and that's probably a conservative estimate).

These books were primarily around the concepts of success, leadership, goal setting, achievement, personal growth, and psychology. I really wanted to know how success was created (funnily enough, most of my reading today is in the same genres). As I read, I noticed that there were often several disconnects between what top achievers did in real life and what the books were advising.

It often became clear which authors were trying to teach something they knew nothing about. Or, as was the case in many situations, which authors had read someone else's publications on success, put their own spin on that author's ideas, and then tried to sell it as their own.

If you really get into the authentic research of personal development, you'll see that many of the materials, books and seminars that exist today are more or less photocopies of someone else's work. That's why it was so important to me to learn first-hand from the real top achievers much in the same way Napoleon Hill did.

As I mentioned, there were also several differences from what top achievers did in real life and the instructions that were being given in the books I read. The books most often were only giving part of the picture. Hopefully, as you've read, you've also noticed a few other things, but right now, I'd like to point out the most significant glaring omission.

Gratitude

I have never seen gratitude appear even in the table of contents in most success books. They primarily focus on goal setting, time management, the psychology of creating more power outcomes, and staying positive in adversity, but no one has really talked about gratitude…

Until now, that is.

In fact, gratitude is such an important component of success that I made a movie about it called *The Gratitude Experiment*. Be sure to check it out.

Here are some important lessons about gratitude and why you need it if you are going to create better outcomes in your life.

Gratitude Expands

When we are grateful for what we already have, it expands and grows. If you are grateful for your existing abundance, you'll soon find that you have more of it. If you're grateful for your relationships, you'll also find that your connections will grow as well.

The contrary is also true. If you neglect and take for granted your abundance, it will shrink and disappear. And if you neglect and take for granted your relationships, they will also disappear or seek connection elsewhere.

One of my students expressed that this was the exact way his divorce was created. As we have taught PPM around the globe, we have seen many marriages and other relationships be saved through understanding this one principle. What you're grateful for expands and grows.

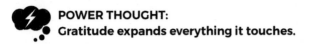

POWER THOUGHT:
Gratitude expands everything it touches.

Gratitude In

As I filmed *The Gratitude Experiment* movie, I had a chance to interview many of today's top thought leaders about the power of gratitude. Some of those who shared their insights with me were Bob Proctor, John Gray (the author of *Men are from Mars, Women are from Venus*), John Demartini, Mary Morrissey, Marie Diamond and others.

As they shared their insights on gratitude, my comprehension of this principle grew, and I realized that I'd pretty much misunderstood it most of my life.

Most people are grateful for what they have in their lives, including gratitude for your house, your car, your bank account, the relationships in your life, your family and friends and so forth. It's known as gratitude out. This is a powerful kind of gratitude, and it certainly makes you thankful for what has happened in your life. But there is a form of gratitude even more powerful.

This mighty form of gratitude is known as gratitude in. This type of gratitude has little to do with anything in your life, but is connected instead to what is inside of you. That is what makes this form of gratitude the more powerful of the two. Gratitude within is based internally, and if something were to interrupt or get between you and things in your life, it would make no difference. This form of gratitude is not dependent on external things or people.

If you lost your house, you would still possess this kind of gratitude. If a loved one died, you could find the gratitude in it. *Gratitude in exists inside of you and is independent.*

As you have learned back when we were discussing the concepts of proactive thinking, you'll recognize that gratitude also can be experienced at different levels. It is like a continuum, and the more it is dependent on others, the less power it has.

Gratitude is a Lens

Earlier in the book, we spoke about perceptions, the lens through which you see the world. Some people have a cynical or negative viewpoint. Others are optimistic. The fastest way to shift to a more empowering view of reality is to see it through the lens of gratitude. When we can observe the world from this perspective, awe and wonder will be more likely to recognize and see opportunities that will help us in our mission. Gratitude is an empowering catalyst for creating powerful change and opening up a process of improvement.

Too often a victim will ask, "Why me?" The result is mental analysis paralysis. Recognizing that each circumstance has an opposite will reveal elements of even the most challenging circumstances, and blessings will be found.

In a recent PPM session I conducted in Las Vegas, I met Trina. Her daughter, Mona, had recently died in an incident involving a drunk driver. It was extremely difficult for her to accept some of the outcomes. Although the driver of the vehicle was in a state of deep remorse, she knew that nothing would bring her daughter back. Trina held on to a massive level of depression.

When she arrived at my PPM event, she expressed that this was her primary reason for coming. She was searching for some kind of release; however, she also expressed that she had tried everything and had begun to lose hope.

Certainly, we acknowledged that nothing would ever take away the pain associated with losing a loved one. That pain, in fact, is part of the gift. Love creates a longing when the relationship is interrupted. Love has many dimensions, and the pain of absence alone is an unbalanced manifestation of love.

As Trina shared her story, we began to explore where gratitude had its place. **Gratitude, in its purest form, is the highest manifestation of love.**

As Trina began to see that there were elements of this situation that were primed with gratitude, she began to experience a greater love for her daughter. She began to see how this experience actually brought her, her family, extended family, other parents who had lost loved ones and many more into a closer relationship with her daughter. She learned that Mona's passing was filled with power and purpose.

As Trina found gratitude in the event and learned how to magnify that gratitude, she was able to find balance in the emotions she had experienced. My greatest gift in participating in this experience was when Trina finally said that her daughter's death "was an event that opened the door for others to find joy, safety and support in their most difficult times."

It was even more powerful for me to learn that on one of our breaks she tracked down the man who had driven his vehicle in a drunken state and killed her daughter. She called him and expressed forgiveness. Together on the phone, they both broke into tears and continued to celebrate what an amazing girl Mona was. Trina learned that the man had felt so bad about Mona's death that he began a blog where he took a firm stand against drunk driving and had made several substantial donations to MADD, or Mothers Against Drunk Driving.

Gratitude doesn't immediately take away pain, but it is a catalyst for regaining balance.

Vision and Maturity

Many of the top achievers I interviewed were more senior to me in age. Age is a funny thing. There is an old saying that talks about how age doesn't matter unless you're a tree. The older we get, the more our perspective changes on certain things. What was once most important to us often becomes trivial later in life.

As we develop a longer-term view of life and a more mature perspective, it is easier to find gratitude in everyday situations. We can also recognize that even the most challenging experiences must succumb to the power of passing time. You've heard some say that when they look back at a challenging time, they will most likely look back and laugh about it, or that looking back the pain of the moment will yield a grand reward. If we bring gratitude more fully into our life, we can speed the separation between the frustration and the fun of events we encounter.

Our grand perspective helps us to recognize that things don't need to be perfect in order for us to begin to experience a sense of gratitude now.

Give Honor to What is Present

Gratitude is best experienced in the present. Remember my earlier chapter about the importance of the present moment? While it is reasonable to feel gratitude for what has passed and is yet to come, *the most powerful gratitude is to experience it in the present.*

Exercise: As you read this book, take a deep breath in. Hold it and release. Be grateful for what is occurring as you breathe. With each breath in, feel more gratitude, do it multiple times until you feel fully charged with gratitude.

Honor the breath that is filling your lungs and imagine it stuffing you with power and light. Each time you do this, feel the intensity grow. You are feeling gratitude in the present.

Consider what you are experiencing at this very moment. What other things can you bring into this same feeling of gratitude? Think of it as a fragile bubble that only you have the power to admit and receive the things of your choosing. Start with the loving of yourself. Feel the powerful, eternal being that you are. Recognize the goodness within and how amazing you really are. Think of your soul and the being of your true self.

Expand beyond that and include the wonder that is your human body. Feel your heart, imagine all the connections of arteries, veins, cells, and structures that must work together, bones and muscles that allow you to move, walk, run and even dance. **What an extraordinary being you are.**

As you do this exercise, continue to expand your field of gratitude beyond yourself. What things in your world can you be grateful for?

Remember, everything that gratitude touches will expand in your life.

Exercise: One of the things that my wife enjoys in our marriage is something that I want to share with you. Now in sharing this, I want to be realistic and let you know immediately that we are not perfect with this idea every night, but as we have done it, it has been a source of power, inspiration, connection and gratitude for us.

We keep a gratitude journal, and while the entries are not long, they are powerful. Each night before we go to bed, we try to end the day with each of us sharing one thing we were most grateful for before we turn in for the night.

If you were to read in our journals, you'd find several reoccurring themes. This has helped us to draw closer to each other as we begin to understand what we each find most valuable in our experiences. For us, the theme of family reappears again and again.

Something else that we like to do and is fun for us is to add pictures to the book. Sometimes we draw them quickly or even add a picture we've taken. As you can imagine, we receive a lot of enjoyment looking back over this journal and revisiting some of these moments.

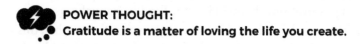

POWER THOUGHT:
Gratitude is a matter of loving the life you create.

Formal Recognition

It is often said when we record something, we remember it better. If we want to have gratitude magnify and be a more obvious part of our life, we must record it. *That which we focus on appears, and that which we give attention to becomes obvious.*

As I have personally spent more time looking for things to be grateful for in my life, gratitude has appeared.

Recently at a session of PPM, I had a couple express to me privately that they wanted to either fix their marriage or call it quits. They had been to several anger management, communication and marriage seminars. They had several ideas that they had tried and most worked for a while, but soon left them back where they started in a dissatisfied, frustrated state. The husband expressed that most of the strategies that they had been given required them to work together as a couple. He continued, "Frankly there are times when we are just so annoyed with each other that working together isn't really an option."

In that statement, he discovered one key to making marriages work. I pointed out that the work should start with them individually. If you bring two people unwilling to see the good in the other and have no trust that the other has the best interest of the marriage at stake, it's tough to make progress. I encouraged them to try an experiment.

If you're experiencing marriage difficulties, you might want to try the same thing here.

Step 1: Make a list of the things you are grateful for about how you behave, do, or bring into the marriage relationship. Do you feel like you are a positive contributor? How so? Find as many things as you can (by the way, don't share this list with your significant other, this is just for you). Make this list daily for the next 30 days. Add to it as needed and carry it around with you referring to it often.

Step 2: Make another list of what you are grateful for that your partner is adding to the relationship. Keep this list and add to it regularly. This one you can share with your significant other as you wish.

Step 3: From time to time, as you both feel inspired to do so, start making a list that each of you will get that expresses what things about the relationship you are grateful for. As you do this, you'll see things begin to shift. If there is a time when your partner isn't willing to participate, that's okay. Just work on your own list.

Gratitude must flow freely and cannot exist in an environment where there is compulsion or manipulation.

Gratitude will Advance your Desires

One of the most common questions I get from attendees of PPM and during interviews I do in the media is how I was able to connect with some of the world's top achievers and most powerful people.

While this may not be the most simplistic answer to give as each situation was unique, I will share that there was one commonality that opened doors and kept them open for future relationships with most of the top achievers.

Obviously, the answer is gratitude. As I expressed gratitude to the top achievers before, during and after our meetings, they were certainly much more willing to support my mission of researching top accomplishers. Because of my sincerity in expressing gratitude, many of them opened doors to other opportunities or even made introductions to other folks I wanted to meet.

Gratitude Can't Coexist with a Taker

Gratitude is an expanding form of energy. It always seeks to move outward and reach further. If an individual is a taker, even if they are saying thank you, the energy is contradictory. It is counter or contrary to what the energy of gratitude really is.

The minute we expand our gratitude to include things beyond ourselves is the moment we begin to experience a shift in how the power of gratitude can support us in achieving our dreams.

If we take a careful look at the universe, everything since the moment of the Big Bang is in expansion mode. When you get into your greatest moments of flow in your life, those moments when it seems like everything is coming together, you are also in some form of expansion.

Gratitude operates the same way. When we resist expansion and growth either through fighting change or being selfish, we are technically fighting against the movement of the universe. Yet when we seek to expand, we are then in harmony with the motion of the universe.

A Group Effort

Often when we talk about experiencing gratitude, we imagine ourselves taking a private moment to meditate or reflect on all the blessings of life. While these private moments may be important, the power of gratitude is magnified when we are connected to others in the experience.

You've probably heard that there is greater synergy in a mastermind when a group is trying to solve a problem. The same is true of the principle of gratitude. As gratitude is experienced in a group, I have seen massive shifts occur in the hearts and minds of people who, through gratitude, become united in a cause, mission or inspiration.

In PPM, one of my favorite and most powerful moments is when the group members take each other by the hands and reflect on what they are most grateful for. Generally speaking, by the time this exercise is complete, there is a powerful sense of unity and connection that is rarely felt elsewhere.

As this power of gratitude is exponentially grown in this circle, people have later expressed how this exercise has helped them to powerfully and inexplicably manifest more of what they were grateful for in their lives. The gratitude circle, as we have come to call it, has been recognized as being responsible for improved relationships, increased abundance, improvements in family situations and promotions at work. The way that these things have occurred has, in fact, been very mysterious and enigmatic. It's almost as if it is magic. And I am surprised almost every single time.

Exercise: I would like to invite you to attend a live session of PPM to experience a gratitude circle. I don't know how else to help you experience this feeling, power and magic except to invite you to be a part of it. At the end of this book are **two free tickets** to a PPM intro near you to help you complete this exercise.

Gratitude is a Celebration

How are you celebrating gratitude in your life? Feelings of gratitude are similar to the same ones that you should feel each time you celebrate something in your life. Gratitude doesn't need to be reserved for moments of meditation. In fact, you should seek out every opportunity to celebrate gratitude in your life. Celebrate the small moments and victories as well as the large ones.

 POWER THOUGHT: Start by being grateful for what is working well and immediately what is working well will start to break down the things that are not.

You'll find that gratitude is also a powerful element of growing your self-worth, self-confidence and self-esteem. As you experience gratitude in your small moments, you'll begin to see that you are truly living a life worth living. You'll recognize more goodness and potential in your situation. You'll be able to dial into your greatest possibilities and have the courage to create more than you ever have before.

As I conclude this chapter, here is a parting thought to consider: while most people define success as freedom, financial freedom, good relationships, a healthy lifestyle, strong self-confidence and worth or one of the other aspects of the five pillars, the one thing that nobody just comes out and asks is, do you love your life?

To me, that is the foundational question of success. How do you really feel about the life you are living? You see, I don't care how much stuff you have or even how healthy you are. If you don't love and are not grateful for your life, you're not creating success at high levels. Now I want to be clear here, I didn't say that you must have a perfect life. We all already understand that things won't go right all the time. But generally speaking, are you truly grateful for and love your life?

That's the purpose. That's the mission. That's the goal. When you feel like you can love the life you have and can have, you are successful.

Questions on the Power of Gratitude to Consider:

1. What is gratitude?

2. What are you grateful for right now?

3. Do you feel blessed at this moment?

4. What are you doing to recognize gratitude in your life?

5. How are you recording gratitude in your life?

6. What are some things that prevent or destroy gratitude?

7. How will gratitude help you get to your goals and dreams?

8. Consider why the energy of gratitude is one of expansion?

9. How are you celebrating gratitude in your life?

CHAPTER ELEVEN

The Power of
Measurement

*Every line is the perfect length
if you don't measure it.*

- Marty Rubin

Measurement is an essential part of improvement

Measurement allows you to delegate

Measurement allows you to spend more time in your brilliance zone

Measurement is the key to creating greater success. When progress is monitored, measured, reported and recognized, it is exponentially multiplied. In life, we only keep track of what's important to us, and we often choose not to measure something when the pain of seeing our status makes us feel bad.

I was reminded of this recently when I was at a family member's house. All the kids in the house began playing on an air hockey table. Those who were winners were always eager to report the score; those on the losing end were insistent that they were just playing for fun, and the score didn't matter.

Contrary to the popular politically correct point of view today, whether a score is assigned or not, success is based on the results you create. *Top achievers do measure, and they do keep score.*

Measurement is an essential part of improvement. If you don't know where you are, you can't calculate what you must do to go further. Often those who don't measure are also saddened to find out that they are building contrary to the things they really want. Time passes, and they are disillusioned to find out that they haven't made any real progress because they haven't measured what they should be doing.

I like what Stephen Covey said in the *7 Habits of Highly Effective People*, "Some people are too busy climbing the ladder to success, and they don't realize it's leaning against the wrong wall." Measurement avoids making that mistake.

 **POWER THOUGHT: We only measure the things that are important to us.**

Measure It to Improve It

Measurement creates an environment where improvement can take place. Most likely you've heard of something called the 80/20 rule. The correct name for this rule is the Pareto Principle. Understanding the history behind this rule may also give you some power in how to use the rule, so I'll share it.

The principle comes from an economist and botanist by the name of Vilfredo Pareto. He lived in Italy in the early 1900s. He first noticed that 80% of the land in Italy was owned by 20% of the population. This concept sparked excitement for him to begin some experimentation.

He began to experiment with potted pea plants and observed from his crop the best 80% of his peas came from 20% of the plants.

Most people stop here with this story and say that 80% of your best will come from 20% of your efforts. Top achievers, however, keep on going much like what Mr. Pareto did. He decided to continue the experiment and nurtured those special 20% high producers to yield another crop. He found that even among that 20% there was also an 80/20 spot of highest producers and those that produced less.

He then split those producers and worked again with the highest special 20% of producers. Again, another 80/20 production. But as you can imagine, he was taking the best of the best of the best, so the production was quite impressive.

Here's the principle: When we measure, we can identify the top 20% that will allow us to refine our best and most productive activities to **refine things even further** with an additional 80/20 split, and measuring that do it again and again until we have really gotten to our highest levels of productivity.

Exercise: Measure your activities (and thinking) to identify your 80/20 split. What are the 20% most productive activities in your day? Among that 20%, what is the 80/20 split, and how can you focus even more precisely on that 20% of the 20%? Is there an even more productive 20% among that 20%? And so on.

Revisit your activities regularly to see if you can go even deeper into your best 20%.

Methods of Measurement

At first glance, most people would imagine that measurement should be focused on specific results. Results that can be numbered and valued are often perceived to be the most important. While specific numbers are very important, remember what we talked about at the beginning of this book in regards to your goals; we also talked about feelings.

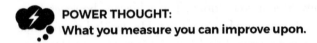

POWER THOUGHT:
What you measure you can improve upon.

Measurement should also include how you feel about what you have achieved. In addition to considering your feelings about what you've achieved, there is a third measurement consideration that should also be essential.

That element of measurement is to **measure your achievements against your highest values**. Are your accomplishments meeting your most esteemed values, and are your continued actions and approaches also meeting those values?

As our values are directly associated with our feelings and sense of fulfillment and satisfaction, they are an important measuring tool.

Delegation

One of the valuable side effects of measurement is that it allows you to recognize what you can delegate and what you must do. If you measure it, you can duplicate it. If you measure it, you can systematize it. **What you don't record and analyze has less significance.**

One of the success interviews that I did early on was with Dr. John Demartini from the movie *The Secret*. John and I have since become very close friends. In chatting with John once about his business growth, he shared with me that several times a year he makes a list of all of the activities that are occupying his time. He then remarks which activities he can delegate to others.

As he grows in his ability to delegate to other people, his business grows. He is freed up to do the highest priority, highest value and highest return activities while the necessities still get done through delegation.

As a result, I have personally found that I can delegate many activities away multiple times throughout the year, thereby freeing myself to do the things I love, and that give me the highest return on my efforts. You'll remember earlier in the book I talked about how many gurus of today would encourage you to step out of your comfort zone to great success. I disagree. Your greatest strength will come from focusing on what you are good at, not uncomfortable with. I call this your brilliance zone.

As you delegate the things that you are uncomfortable with, you will be able to spend more time in your brilliance zone. As a result, your productivity and profitability will increase exponentially. **Daily practice creates exponential improvement.**

Accountability Plan

Accountability is one of the reasons why most people never succeed. They know what they want and even have a significant emotional attachment to it. What they are lacking is accountability. There are several ways to create accountability. The following aspects are the ones that I have found to be most successful for people who have been through our program:

A planner: I have observed that if people merely think about an activity, it rarely gets accomplished. If they make a plan around that activity, it sometimes gets accomplished. If they schedule it, it gets done. It is essential that you schedule any activities that you wish to get done. **Your planner is your best accountability partner**, and what I call the first line of defense.

If you do not build a daily schedule, you are bound to be interrupted daily. If you can't take control of your day, you will be controlled by everything around you. Most people today use some form of an electronic planner, and if that works for you, go for it. I have found that most top achievers still like to use a written diary. It just seems like it is faster and more convenient and easier to update as changes happen. I also like the idea of writing things down, as it implants it more firmly in my memory.

Side note: We have developed a fantastic version of a planner specifically for use with the principles of PPM. This planner is equipped with a system to help you maintain focus and prioritize tasks in a way that will help you get to your goals quicker. In addition, we have added specific teaching and tools that help you learn and apply the PPM principles at a deeper level in your life in real time. If you would like to get access to one of these planners go to www.PersonalPowerMastery.com and click on Store.

A study group: Surrounding yourself with other like-minded people is a brilliant way to improve your chances of creating powerful outcomes. Masterminds and study groups are powerful ways to learn the PPM content and to add to your power to achievements. Masterminds and study groups also open new ways of looking at the content and expanding your understanding of key concepts and principles.

In most of the cities where PPM has been offered in the past, study groups exist to help you implement the lessons from the training. In many cases, these study groups are conducted by our certified coaches, and are in and of themselves a very powerful experience.

If you are interested in starting a study group in your area, please reach out to us, and we can share some circular materials for you to use alongside this book or what you have learned at a live training. Reach out to my assistant Rachel Dobson to get started: rachel@douglasvermeeren.com.

A coach: As I mentioned above, utilizing our certified coaches is a brilliant way to exponentially increase your success with the PPM materials. These coaches are trained in effective ways of helping you stay accountable and achieve more. You can find one of our certified coaches through our official website www.PersonalPowermastery.co or attending a live training in your area.

One of the big advantages of using one of our certified coaches is that they can help you with lessons, exercises and strategies that they learned from our exclusive training sessions. These tools are designed specifically to help you go deeper than any of the training you may have experienced up to that point.

You can certainly understand the difference between reading this book and working with a coach week after week on implementing the material in real time. This is where some of our greatest success stories happen. Naturally, we would love to include your future successes among the differences we are making to people just like you around the world.

Another side note: If you're interested in being trained as one of our certified trainers, we are looking for you! To apply, reach out to

Rachel Dobson at rachel@douglasvermeeren.com

Daily journal: Use a daily journal to record and measure your success. You can use any journal or notebook for this journey, but you do need to come up with a structure that works for you. Record each day with your activities and measure them against your goals and values. For increased and accelerated success, I recommend using one of our official PPM journals because of the added tools.

How Would Others Measure Against Your Values?

As I go around the world speaking with different groups, I share the stage with many successful speakers. In fact, this weekend I was speaking at an event in Las Vegas and there were some extremely famous, successful and well-known speakers that spoke at this event. Chances are very, very good that you know some of the power names that were there.

As I waited in the green room for my opportunity on the stage, I looked around and was in awe of some of the amazing people speaking that day. It was very easy to begin to think of the massive accomplishment of some of these people. As I looked around the room, I noticed one well-known speaker who had built an empire of success.

He was not only extremely famous, but he was also extremely wealthy and successful. In many aspects, he was much farther ahead than me. I almost began to feel a bit intimidated. That was until I began to talk with him, and while I still admire him, I quickly felt that many of our values were not aligned.

The things that he had sacrificed to become who he was were things that I would not be willing to sacrifice. As we spoke, I could see there were things he longed for from my life.

As I began to recognize how different our values were, and how each of us had created according to our highest values, I realized that there was no need for jealousy or comparison.

You'll remember earlier in the book I pointed out that criticism, jealousy and competition are all manifestations of scarcity thinking. **Scarcity thinking is not an expanding force but a constricting one.** It never creates a good situation or improves a bad one.

Albert Einstein once said, "Not everything that counts can be counted, and not everything that's counted truly counts." *Let your measurement be a true reflection of what is most important to you and connected directly to your values.*

Comparison to others is certainly one of the fastest ways to feel inadequate about yourself and your accomplishments. Yet it is one of the hardest things to refrain from doing. Our society is on the constant alert to cause us to see what others around us are achieving and accomplishing. Even in work situations, we are often being compared to our peers or even asked to compete in contests and competitions. I understand that competition can often bring out a higher level of ourselves. I am not *against* competition, but competition is truly about measuring yourself against a task rather than against an individual. If you win or lose, much more is revealed about you personally in the long run than will ever be exposed between you and another individual.

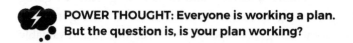

POWER THOUGHT: Everyone is working a plan. But the question is, is your plan working?

To win any competition, the first thing you need to do is realize that you are your only opponent. There is a samurai saying that says, "When you defeat the enemy within, no enemy without can harm you."

Focus on gaining control over yourself, and you'll find that no other victory will bring you the same kind of peace.

A True Master Never Stops Improving

Perfectionism is a myth. Top achievers know it doesn't exist. Instead of seeking perfection, they are improvisers always experimenting and exploring. Top achievers never wait to have all the answers, and any answers they receive, they attempt to make improvements with them.

All the top achievers that I interviewed were on the hunt for how improvements could be made. Often the improvements they made were very small things that most people would overlook or ignore. But these top achievers recognized that the great advantages and successes were created in the smallest details.

When I first began training in Brazilian Jiu-Jitsu, I envied those who were much further along than me. In fact, I remember one day looking at one of our professors who had attained his black belt several years ago. I thought that it must be nice to know everything there is to know about Jiu-Jitsu. At times I also wished that I had started much earlier so I could be where he was now. I recognize now that I was wrong with both of my feelings.

Mastery is a journey, and I have discovered along the way there are so many memories, benefits and tools I am gaining by going through the training in the very moment that I am doing it. Truth be known, some things are especially more enjoyable and valuable because they are lessons I am learning right now. Had I received them earlier or learned them without the effort, they wouldn't be as valuable to me, and they wouldn't give me the same kind of excitement or pleasure I am now receiving because of their proper arrival.

Secondly, as I have now grown in the martial arts, I have seen that the adage is true. The more I learn, the more I realize I don't know. I have many black belt friends now, and each of them shares the same sentiment that the more experience they gain, the more the world of Jiu-Jitsu opens to them.

 POWER THOUGHT: Our happiness is directly attached to our feelings of progress and improvement.

Mastery then, in my opinion, is no longer about becoming the expert. It is more about becoming a better student. The more you learn, the more you wish to learn. The more knowledge you take in, the better the questions you can ask. The more education you gain, the more your journey becomes exciting.

Recognize Your Growth

Oftentimes, people struggle to feel good about what they have created because they fail to *recognize* what they have created. **Sometimes practice happens so slow it can't be recognized, and other times, even when it happens fast, it is not always recognized by the person making progress**. Others may or may not see it, but the person who is making progress seldom sees it.

Measurement allows you to recognize the progress you are making and steer those results and activities to more progress.

One of the most important aspects of growth includes recognizing and rewarding your growth. Top achievers do not take for granted that they have done a good job. They attach great rewards to their efforts, and generally, those rewards can be big motivating factors to prime them to accomplish greater and greater things.

This has been a powerful tool to fight against procrastination for many of our students. As they have positioned their rewards on the other side of specific benchmarks they were looking to achieve, they found more power to get started, stay focused and get the job done.

Remember the mantra expressed by many of the top achievers: "Get the worst done first." Completing the tasks you know you need to do isn't always easy or fun, but there are massive rewards in the end. However, it is often difficult to get yourself motivated just because of rewards at the end. Sometimes those rewards are so far distant that they don't really get us all that excited. When you position your rewards closer to the completion of each task, those tasks just become easier to do.

Exercise: Consider what rewards are exciting and valuable to you. Make a list of rewards that mean something to you and attach them specifically to benchmarks and activities that you are struggling to accomplish. Promise yourself that as you stretch to reach higher and higher, you will reward yourself with these rewards.

One of our students, Timothy, struggled with knowing what he wanted, but not getting to work to make any of it happen. Most of the time he confessed that it came down to not scheduling the activities. Once he attached some of his rewards to the activities, he found himself looking for more opportunities to get out and get to work. In fact, this became so successful for him, he began to take his entire Friday as his reward day. He began to experience so much success earlier in the week that he ultimately ended up including Thursday too. That meant every week he had a four-day weekend. He could do it because he started getting so much done at the beginning of the week, he could take the balance of the week off with ease.

When I spoke with him about his progress and looked at what he achieved, he surprised me by getting more done in a day of focused work than most people got done in a week or more of unfocused work.

POWER THOUGHT: The success story that is you is being written right now. What are you including in your story?

One of the top achievers that I interviewed shared that he gave himself a major reward every three months. He would work at a very high and focused level for two and a half months and then take two weeks of vacation to wherever he and his family wanted to go, which equated to taking eight weeks or two months off every year.

The same top achievers shared this mantra: "Work hard, play hard." He was a strong example of being able to do both and still maintain an extremely high level of productivity and balance.

Plan for the Future

Measurement allows you to plan for the future. Most people plan in part as a result of the regrets that they have. Often, they look at their life and simply say that they don't want to experience what they had or what they created again. When you plan and use the deliberate act of measurement and evaluation, your plan will come from a different place. It will be a deliberate choice of seeking out and creating the outcomes that you truly value and the future that ultimately has you excited.

The future is yours, and measurement puts that future more intentionally in your hands. Nothing will be an accident, and you will see the level of your results rise with your desires and ambitions.

Patterns

Patterns in your life are directly attached to the results you will achieve. Often if you haven't established a pattern, you will not get consistent results in the long term. By evaluation and measurement, you can recognize what patterns were used to create the results you are currently experiencing, and how your current patterns can be improved to create better results.

Perspective

When you keep a good measurement of your life, you have a much more powerful perspective of who you are, where you've been, and where you're going. Perspective is one of the most powerful attributes of top achievers. Perspective is much more than simply a vantage point from which to observe what is going on. It is a sense of power that you can use to gain control over every aspect of your life. As we present this as one of the final components of PPM, I am always amazed at how this gift of perspective is so closely linked to the very first thing we talked about in this book and in the course. Perspective does open the door to a proper connection to you.

Perspective is one of the most powerful ways of making your success personal. As you gain broader perspective, you expand and grow. You become a more fulfilled and balanced individual. Your sense of joy, happiness, completeness and satisfaction all expand. Your ability to feel confident about yourself and your mission also grow.

If you think life is difficult, you'll see it shift as your perspective does.

As you gain a deeper perspective of who you are, and how you fit into all that is, you begin to experience more of all that is. You begin to connect more completely with your purpose and every other being on the planet. Perspective is one of the greatest gifts you will ever receive.

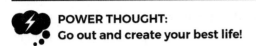 **POWER THOUGHT:**
Go out and create your best life!

Questions on the Power of Measurement to Consider:

1. Why is it important to measure?

2. What should you measure?

3. How will you measure it?

4. How does the 80/20 rule influence your success?

5. How are you improving your life with the understanding of the 80/20 rule?

6. How are you measuring?

7. Are you measuring against specifics and your feelings?

8. Are you measuring against your values?

9. What can you delegate to others?

10. How are you recording your measurements?

11. How can you start a study group to help you gain greater success?

12. How are you using a mentor or coach to measure your progress?

13. Why is it dangerous to measure against the success of others?

14. Why should you measure against your values?

15. What purpose does jealousy serve?

16. How do your activities measure against your values?

17. How are you recognizing and rewarding your improvements?

18. How are you measuring your future?

19. What details can be improved?

CONCLUSION

Now you have had a brief glimpse of some of the key principles of Personal Power Mastery. I thank you for taking the time to enter the exciting world of top achievers. As I discovered these rules for a more successful life and more powerful outcomes, my entire life has changed. The efforts haven't always been easy, but the rewards have been astonishing.

I encourage you to seek ways to implement what you have learned in this book. I can promise you that if you do you will experience more freedom, opportunity and satisfaction in your life.

Will you remember the five pillars of success that we talked about near the beginning of this book? Self, spirituality, health, relationships and abundance. I have seen marvelous, miraculous changes and improvements in the lives of people from all over the world as they have implemented these lessons into their own life in real time.

Don't just read this book – live it. If you do, doors will open and blessings pour in.

As I do at the end of each of our live sessions, I encourage you to share your stories directly with me. You can contact me at doug@douglasvermeeren.com

Final Steps

My call to action has always been for you to live this book, not just read it. So here are a few suggestions of things you can do right now to increase the probability that you will succeed with the materials outlined in this book:

1. **Attend a live session of PPM.** There are so many more tools, strategies and insights I want to share with you to create your own PPM. Some of these things are very difficult to teach and experience in a book. When you attend and re-attend PPM you'll recognize a new-found power in your life that can only be gained through the experiential activities that you will participate in. Set this as a goal and then re-attend to sharpen your saw again and again.

2. **Seek out a certified PPM coach.** This is a powerful way to gain more accountability in your life. If you have one of our coaches supporting you on your journey, success will arrive so much quicker. Our coaches are trained to help you, and they can quickly recognize shortcuts you can take to creating your success.

3. **Join or start a study group in your area.** One of the most fascinating things I have seen over my years of teaching PPM is how much easier it is to create your personal success if you are surrounded by like-minded people who believe in you and can help you mastermind your efforts to creating success. As mentioned earlier we have lots of great resources and tools for those in masterminds and study groups, and I am eager to support you.

One last thought that I wanted to share with you is that I have often thought about what the most important message was that I learned in my time with the world's top achievers. In my interactions with them, this is still the most important message that I want to share with you:

As we part ways for a time, I want you to always remember that you are brilliant. You are a unique individual with powerful gifts to bring to the world. Whatever your past may be or where you came from, you are just one new choice away from a completely different ending.

This is the reason I do this work. I remember how I felt in the presence of truly amazing people. You are one of those people. I look forward to meeting you soon to celebrate your success. The mission of a top achiever really comes down to helping others discover their greatness.

When you start to realize just how amazing you are, pass it on and help someone discover the same thing about themselves.

ADDITIONAL RESOURCES

Here are some additional resources with some great free tools for you to expand your understanding and application of Personal Power Mastery.

Personal Power Mastery Podcast

Search: Personal Power Mastery – This weekly podcast is something many of my students love to take with them on their phone or smart device. On each episode I share additional insights and strategies for implementing Personal Power Mastery in your daily life, I also bring on guests from time to time and we talk about how the principles in Personal Power Mastery have helped them create success. You can find a link to the podcast through my website or on the following networks: Google Play, Player FM, SoundCloud, Stitcher, Tunein, iHeartRadio, Spotify and iTunes, (and most likely others by the time of this printing).

Personal Power Mastery weekly YouTube show

Search: Douglas Vermeeren #PPM - This weekly YouTube show answers specific questions from participants of Personal Power Mastery, features special guest top achievers, shares and explores deeper material and provides insights into daily application of Personal Power Mastery.

Personal Power Mastery Facebook group

Group name: Personal Power Mastery with Douglas Vermeeren - In this group I share articles, videos, quotes and answer questions in real time almost every day. It is a great international community to belong to that will support you in your journey to personal mastery. **Link: https://www.facebook.com/groups/2031818787056244/**

Twitter

I tweet lots of cool stuff including news and event information. I use my twitter to also share daily quotes and lots of other fun stuff. Be sure to come and join me.

Twitter: @DougVermeeren

Instagram

I share lots of pictures from things going on and other top achievers I meet. If you like to bump into celebrities and top achievers you'll like my Instagram. I also share quotes and tips that you'll find valuable.

Instagram: DouglasVermeeren

My Website

My website has tons of resources, videos, clips from my media appearances, articles and so much more. In addition, the above links are all there and many more with free and paid tools to help you create Personal Power Mastery in your life.

Link: www.DouglasVermeeren.com

You can also get us directly at 1-877-393-9496 or email me directly at doug@douglasvermeeren.com, I'd love to hear from you.

MY GIFT TO YOU

2 FREE TICKETS TO PPM

$5997 Value

I want to see you at the next Personal Power Mastery Event! And I'll cover your ticket!

Use this code to register for **2 free tickets** to a

Personal Power Mastery
3 day session near you for FREE

VIP Registration code: **PPMbook123**
to register call: 1-877-393-9496

ABOUT THE AUTHOR

What would you do with the secrets of the world's top achievers? Would you level up your income? Your business? Your opportunities? Now you can find out because those secrets are now available to you.

Over the last two decades Douglas Vermeeren has conducted extensive first-hand research into the lives of the world's top achievers. He has the success strategies of top business leaders from Nike, Reebok, Fruit of the Loom, FedEx, KFC, United Airlines, Microsoft, Disney and others to share with you. ABC television and FOX Business refer to him as the modern-day Napoleon Hill.

In addition, he is the producer and director of three out of ten of the top personal development movies ever made. He is the producer of *The Opus* (featuring Jack Canfield, Mark Victor Hansen, Joe Vitale, John Demartini, Marci Shimoff, Morris Goodman, Bob Doyle and others); *The Gratitude Experiment* (Bob Proctor, Marie Diamond, John Demartini, John Gray); and *The Treasure Map* (John Demartini, Loral Langemeier, Raymond Aaron, Marshall Sylver, Randy Gage).

Douglas has authored three books in the Guerrilla Marketing series and is the creator of Personal Power Mastery, which has been consistently rated as one of the top events for personal change and development worldwide.

He is a regular featured expert on FOX, CNN, ABC, NBC, CTV, CBC, The Huffington Post, NY Daily News and others.

For more info go to www.DouglasVermeeren.com